Classic Racing Cars

Hamlyn
London·New York
Sydney·Toronto

Classic
Racing Cars
Cyril Posthumus

Acknowledgements

The author wishes to thank Derek Gardner of Tyrrell, Gordon Coppuck of McLaren, Denis Jenkinson and Doug Nye for their information and help in unravelling knotty problems, and many magazines, manufacturers and people for help with illustrations.

The publishers are grateful to the following for the illustrations in this book: Alfa Romeo; James Allington; Associated Press; *Autocar*; Bill Bennett: Diana Burnett; Jerry Chesebrough; Fiat; Ford; G. Gédo; Geoff Goddard, Hamlyn Group; Brian Hatton; David Hodges; B. Hoeppner; Indianapolis Motor Speedway; Louis Klemantaski; Lancia; James Leech; Matra; Mercedes-Benz; *Motor*; *Motor Sport*; Phipps Photographic; John Player Team Lotus; Cyril Posthumus; *Road & Track*; Nigel Snowdon; Team Lotus; Texaco; Robert P. Tronolone; Michael Turner

Published by The Hamlyn Publishing Group Limited
London · New York · Sydney · Toronto
Astronaut House, Feltham, Middlesex, England
Copyright © The Hamlyn Publishing Group Limited, 1977
Second Impression 1978

ISBN 0 600 31909 1

Filmset by Tradespools Limited, Frome, Somerset
Printed in Hong Kong

Contents

Introduction

Of the first class, of allowed excellence . . . (and much more) says the Oxford Concise dictionary of the word 'classic', but in motor racing, albeit sometimes harshly, success is a further vital criterion. Every car of the 40 chosen for this book has won at least one race and possesses other merits which, I feel, justify its inclusion. Some readers may disagree, some may protest indignantly at seemingly unjust omissions. To admirers of the Bentley, Jaguar and the like, I hasten to emphasise that 'racing cars' in this book mean out-and-out racing cars devoid of mudguards, lights, a second (empty) seat and other trappings that feature on what are loosely termed 'sports-racing cars'. To devotees of the ERA, Ballot, Type 51 or 59 Bugatti, B-type Connaught, 8CM Maserati and numerous other fine cars, I can but offer the defence that quart-into-pint pot measures will only go so far, reserving the hope that, should reaction to this book be encouraging enough, the publishers may follow up with another, remedying such omissions.

Still on the defensive, some comment on the specifications seems advisable. In earlier days when Grands Prix were few and cars raced but rarely, a maximum road speed meant something and is therefore quoted. In modern times, with well over a dozen major races in one well-packed season, over a wide variation of circuits commanding different drive ratios, to offer an estimated maximum speed is pointless—and often impossible. I am compelled, moreover, to hide behind that comforting word 'approximate' in several other statistics, particularly those of brake horsepower. On the door of one of the dynamometer cells at John Nicholson's Hounslow works, where Cosworth-Ford DFV engines are prepared for

the McLaren Formula 1 team, there hung until recently a notice which put the problem in a nutshell. It said:

Bhp = 60 per cent perspiration
10 per cent inspiration
10 per cent constipation
20 per cent manipulation.

Just after the Second World War there were jokes about generous 'Maserati horsepower' (and of how it was all too readily dissipated *outside* the crankcase of over-stressed 4CLs), but that famous marque was far from being the only culprit in the 'paper horsepower' race. When seeking data for this book I frequently found two or three different bhp figures quoted for an engine, ranging from cheerful round figures of, say, 300bhp to the suspiciously meticulous 292·5bhp. In his notebooks the late Laurence E. Pomeroy was wont to append the letters *cgs* after some power figures; they denoted *cum grano salis*, or 'with a pinch of salt', an excellent proviso in some instances, one feels. In any case, quoting the inimitable words of that great racing mechanic Alfons Francis, 'it's what gets to the bloddy back wheels that counts'.

Even wheelbase and track dimensions are not exempt from doubt. Famous scale model builder Rex Hays, who ran his tape measure over leading racing cars whenever the chance came, declared that he frequently found discrepancies, sometimes in excess of 2 inches, from the makers' officially-stated figures. With 'tolerance' in such cases clearly meaning more than the '1½ or 2 thou' of precision engineering, I therefore crave a little tolerance for the statistics offered, even though every effort has been made to ensure accuracy.

C.P.

1906 Grand Prix Renault

'Ah—Szisz on the Renault—what a spectacle! A blast on the bugle, it is he, he is past, a red whirlwind—gone!'

Frantz Reichel, 'Les Sports Modernes', 1906

If Grand Prix-winning cars are the acme of design enterprise, as might well be expected, then the 1906 Renault will seem disappointing. For its time it was dully conventional – a side-valve four-cylinder, three-speed machine with homely 'alligator' bonnet, high wheels and narrow track – yet through sheer high speed stamina it outpaced technically more advanced rivals to win the first French Grand Prix, a gruelling two-day affair at Le Mans, by over 32 minutes. It was materially helped by its makers' foresight in fitting a new type detachable wheel rim which saved vital minutes in tyre changing, yet its sternest rivals, the Italian Fiats, enjoyed the same benefit. They also had overhead valves, an extra 3·2 litres and 20 more bhp, but could not match the French car's pace.

When the Automobile Club de France announced their new race, as a successor to the Gordon Bennett series with its frustrating entry limit of three cars per nation, Renault Frères of Billancourt were among the seven French manufacturers which entered teams.

Fiat and Itala from Italy and Mercedes of Germany also came, most of them with 1905 Gordon Bennett pattern cars. But the 1905 Renaults, though enterprisingly different with underslung chassis and semi-unitary chassis/body construction, had suffered dire cooling troubles and so were scrapped in favour of all-new Grand Prix cars costing about £10000 each in 1906 money. These reverted to higher built conventional channel-steel chassis and thermosyphon cooling as on Renault production models.

The massive, simple, side-valve four-cylinder engines from the earlier cars were retained. Their iron cylinders with fixed heads were cast in pairs, with copper water jackets silver-soldered around them. Bore and stroke were 'oversquare' at 166 × 150mm (12986cc), there was a single Renault up-draught carburetter feeding through a two-branch manifold, and the latest Simms-Bosch high-tension magneto with automatic advance was employed. Engine output of 90 bhp at 1200 rpm was modest by com-

The shape of 70 years ago – one of the three 13-litre Renaults which contested the first Grand Prix at Le Mans in 1906. Its driver, Edmond, had a particularly harrowing time, breaking his goggles on lap 3, and having to give up the race in agony through tar getting in his eyes. Another Renault crashed, but Szisz made no mistake about winning by over half an hour from Nazzaro's Fiat

parison with the 110bhp of the Fiats and Clément-Bayards. As on every Renault ever made since the first one in 1898, the drive passed through a separate three-speed gearbox to the rear wheels via a clean, quiet propellor shaft and live axle rather than oily, threshing exposed chains. The characteristic Renault scuttle-mounted radiator and rear-hinged bonnet probably had better penetration than the severely upright nose radiators of the opposition, and certainly allowed the driver a better view of the road.

Semi-elliptic leaf springing was used all round, giving a fairly soft ride assisted by probably the first double-acting hydraulic shock absorbers ever used in a race, invented and patented by Louis Renault himself. The two bucket seats seemed ludicrously high after the low-built 1905 cars, but the designers spurned the usual ugly cylindrical fuel tank, employing instead a neat reservoir forming the tail of the car, straddled by three spare tyres and rims. National racing colours were not essential, and the Renaults looked particularly effective in bright red, with bright brass bonnet 'bevels' and fittings.

On the weighbridge the winner's car scaled 990kg, comfortably below the top limit of 1007kg (2220lb) and lightest of all the serious contenders, three speeds instead of four and final drive minus a differential helping to keep weight down. The triangular

64·1-mile Sarthe circuit was rough in parts with a sharp, flinty surface supposedly bound by tar but promising to break up under stress or hot weather. Before race day, therefore, Renault changed their wire wheels for new Michelin wood-spoked artillery type, the rear pairs having detachable rims. These were the celebrated *jantes amovibles*, the new 1906 answer to the puncture problem that dogged every motorist in those days.

The wheel rims were retained through eight steel wedges held in place by nuts. When these were undone with a brace, the whole tyre on its separate steel rim came away from the felloe of the wheel proper, whereupon a new tyre, ready-inflated, could be bolted on. Two wheels could be changed by two people in under four minutes, whereas changing the normal security-bolted tyre could take four times as long, even using the 'knife and muscle' method which entailed cutting the tyre away bodily, levering on a new one and inflating the tube from a cylinder – an exhausting, time-wasting job which only the driver and his riding mechanic were allowed to perform by the ACF's rules.

That pioneer Grand Prix proved a tremendous test of men and machinery, being much more like a Le Mans GP d'Endurance than a modern 1½-hour 'sprint GP'. Contestants had to cover 12 laps overall, or 769·4 miles, split over two days with the cars

Although rugged in build, the Grand Prix Renault weighed under a ton. The radiator behind the engine and 'alligator' engine cover were Renault characteristics; the huge flywheel and cone clutch behind the engine transmitted to the separate three-speed gearbox. The rear-mounted fuel tank held about 30 gallons, and minimum consumption was about 7mpg. The Michelin detachable wheel rims, which were a deciding factor in the race, were fitted to the rear wheels only in 1906, but all round in 1907–08

locked up overnight in a *parc fermé*. Tropical weather with a noon temperature reaching 120 degrees in the sun made things worse, but Ferenc, Franz or Francois Szisz, an Austro-Hungarian who was Renault's chief test driver, set a fast, heady pace from the start. He moved ahead on lap three, extending the Renault on the straight (his 92·43 mph through a flying kilometre was fastest of all 32 runners) and drew out a lead of over 26 minutes on the first day from a Clément-Bayard and a Fiat.

With the same exhausting heat and a circuit that was breaking up fast, it was clearly 'a race of tyres' on the second day. Following his earlier tactics, Szisz remained unassailable despite several punctures when the Michelin rims proved invaluable. Both his team mates had to retire, and drama came on the penultimate lap when the surviving Renault broke a rear spring, but Szisz made good use of a 46-minute lead and 'pussy-footed' home to victory ahead of Nazzaro's Fiat. In all the winner made nine stops for tyres, yet averaged 62·88 mph in a gruelling race which lasted him 12 hours 14 minutes 7 seconds. An unexpectedly fast, durable car, an intelligent driver, and excellent pit-work had saved France's face and prevented her first Grand Prix from falling to Italy. The Austro-Hungarian followed up his Sarthe triumph with second place in the following year's Grand Prix, this time *behind* a Fiat, and the by then well outdated GP Renault's last race was the American Grand Prize of 1908, when Szisz lay fourth until a wheel bearing failed and he had to retire.

Specification
Engine
Four cylinders, in-line; bore and stroke, 166 × 150 mm; capacity, 12986 cc; side valves; Renault carburetter; Simms-Bosch h-t magneto; maximum power, 90 bhp at 1200 rpm.
Transmission
Separate three-speed gearbox and propellor shaft.
Chassis
Channel-steel side members; semi-elliptic leaf springs front and rear; Renault hydraulic dampers. Internal expanding rear brakes and transmission brake. Michelin detachable rims and tyres.
Dimensions
Wheelbase, 9ft 6·25in; front track, 4ft 5·2in; rear track, 4ft 2·5in; dry weight, 2183lb.
Maximum speed
94 mph.

1907 Grand Prix Fiat

'Our national pride is deeply touched. A race won is a battle won—a battle by industry, won by engines, by courage, by organisation . . . '

Corriere della Sera, 1907

Second place was not good enough for Giovanni Agnelli, dynamic chief of the Fabbrica Italiana Automobili Torino, a vigorous concern determined to put their Fiat car and Italy on the International racing map. They began, like many, by copying the radical new Mercedes in 1902–03, but quickly developed an independent character which, coupled with spirited Latin driving, took them right into the big league. They tackled the Gordon Bennett race in 1904 with 75hp T-head side-valve cars without success, but in 1905 Nazzaro and Cagno with new 100hp overhead-valve cars took second and third places to the winning Brasier. Then came France's first Grand Prix in 1906 and another second to Nazzaro, backed up by yet another second by Lancia in America's Vanderbilt Cup race. Agnelli was pleased, but still wanted outright victory.

In 1907 he got it in intoxicating measure. Nazzaro won, not one, but *three* major races, the Targa Florio in Sicily, the Kaiser's Cup in Germany, and the French Grand Prix at Dieppe! For his first two wins Nazzaro drove *corsa* derivatives of basically touring model Fiats, but for the all-important Grand Prix

the 1905–06 100hp racers were rebuilt. Beneath their Mercedes-style exteriors these Fiats were the first serious exponents of overhead valves and hemispherical cylinder heads in racing. Designers were groping for an effective overhead valve arrangement, and the Fiat approach was an elaboration of the Mercedes overhead inlet system.

From a gear-driven camshaft in the crankcase, each pair of valves was operated by a single pushrod and a large single rocker, much drilled for lightness. A half-elliptic triple-leaf spring on a central pivot closed both valves, the inlets of which were of unusual 'annular' type as pioneered by Mercedes in 1903, with perforations which admitted extra gas when the valve was open, but were blanked off when closed. The four sparking plugs were central in the hemispherical heads, ignition was by Simms-Bosch low-tension magneto, and there was a single carburetter. The bore and stroke dimensions of this great unit were oversquare at 180×160mm, giving the impressive capacity of 16286cc.

Designer of the engine was Giovanni Enrico, although a similar valve gear had

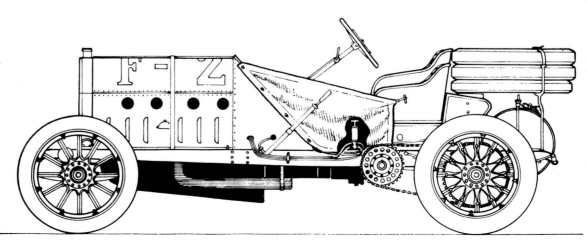

Lofty profile of the early Grand Prix racer is typified by the winning Fiat of 1907. Its 9ft 4in wheelbase accommodated the huge 16·3-litre engine, two seats for driver and mechanic, and a rear fuel tank, over which the spare wheel rims and tyres were strapped

been patented in 1902 by a young Frenchman, Emile Petit, whose later 1921 Salmson 'four-pushrod' 1100cc engine also followed the principle. When Enrico left Fiat in 1906 his successors Guido Fornaca and Carlo Cavalli began a stern quest for more power. They modified the valve gear, improved the manifolding and lubrication, and stepped up crankshaft speed from 1100 to 1600rpm and output from 110 to 130bhp. They retained Enrico's multiple-disc wet clutch and four-speed gearbox, and also the 1905 chassis with its chain drive, braking on the rear wheels and transmission, and wooden artillery wheels with detachable rims as used in the 1906 Grand Prix.

Admirably epitomising the 'monster' age of racing cars, the big red 130hp Fiat weighed fractionally over a ton dry. Its huge flat-top cast-iron pistons, over 7in in diameter, weighed over 10lb each, a single connecting rod scaled over 14lb, two men could barely lift the three-bearing crankshaft and flywheel, yet ironically the control levers and pedals were painstakingly drilled to save a few ounces. The engine discharged into a huge exhaust pipe some 4·5in in diameter, while at the rear a big cylindrical fuel tank taking 44 UK gallons was mounted low between the chassis side members. The ACF imposed a fuel consumption limit for 1907 of 30 litres per 100km – approximately 9·4mpg – tanks being filled before the start and the rest going to the pits in sealed cans.

A more popular ACF measure was to cut race duration from the over-long 1906 two-day affair to a one-day race over 10 laps of a 47·74-mile circuit outside Dieppe. Oddly, Fiat's three-car entry came in late at double fees of £400 each, but 'the last shall be first' virtually summed up their fortunes, for they won the ballot for starting places, Lancia was first away on July 2nd, 1907, and Nazzaro was first home, just over 6¾ hours later. Louis Wagner in the third Fiat had led the first three laps, then retired, after which Lancia and Nazzaro climbed up to second and third positions until Lancia's car dropped back with trouble. The 27-year-old Nazzaro then found himself at grips for first place with his 1906 adversary, Szisz on the Renault, but this time the overhead valve Fiat had the legs of the French side-valve car. Implacably the Fiat moved ahead and Felice Nazzaro, *le Metronome* to his countrymen for his superbly precise driving, won the Grand Prix at 70·5mph by over six minutes, climaxing *l'anno d'oro* for himself, for Fiat, and for Italy. Behind him ran 15 French cars and one German. . . .

Specification
Engine
Four cylinders, in-line; bore and stroke, 180 × 160mm; capacity, 16286cc; overhead valves operated by four pushrods; two valves per cylinder at 60 degrees; single carburetter; Simms-Bosch l-t magneto; maximum power 130bhp at 1600rpm.
Transmission
Separate four-speed gearbox and open side chains.
Chassis
Channel-steel side members; semi-elliptic leaf springs front and rear; drum-type friction dampers. Internal expanding rear brakes and transmission band brake. Michelin detachable rims and tyres.
Dimensions
Wheelbase, 9ft 4in; track, 4ft 5·2in front and rear; dry weight, 2242lb.
Maximum speed
103mph.

Below: *advanced for its time, the 180 × 160mm four-cylinder Fiat engine had overhead valves operated by pushrods and huge rockers. The Simms-Bosch low-tension magneto is gear driven*

Bottom: *ready for the fray – 1907 Grand Prix winner Felice Nazzaro guides his Fiat out to the starting line. Alongside, on right, is his team mate Vincenzo Lancia, who lost third place through clutch trouble on the last lap*

1908 Grand Prix Mercedes

'He cornered as though on the end of a piece of string, not losing an atom of ground.'

'La Vie au Grand Air'

If the 1907 Grand Prix was a humbling defeat in the eyes of chauvinist Frenchmen, then the 1908 race over the same Dieppe circuit rated a positive disaster. The field of 48 starters included 24 French cars representing eight separate teams, yet of the first seven cars to finish the 477·5-mile race, six were German, with the best French entry fourth, and the next eighth!

The winning car was a 12·8-litre Mercedes, designed by Paul Daimler and driven by Christian Lautenschlager, foreman tester at the factory. It was the triumphant culmination of much determined effort by the Stuttgart marque, whose last major victory came in the 1903 Gordon Bennett race. They had tried hard in the 1907 Grand Prix with three 175 × 150mm, 14·4-litre big-fours, but could only manage 10th place. As the 1908 event was staged over the same course, the methodical Germans, who had logged all relevant data concerning its 47·75-mile lap, tried again – and had test cars circulating at Dieppe three months beforehand.

New regulations imposed a top bore limit of 155mm for four-cylinder cars and a minimum weight of 1100kg (2420lb), which meant building new engines. Fixing the bore at 154·7mm, Mercedes chose a lengthy stroke of 170mm (180mm on one car intended as pacemaker!), which gave 12·8 litres and 135bhp at 1400rpm. Trusting proven principles rather than the new-fangled overhead valves, they adhered to their old system of twin camshafts in the crankcase, one operating the overhead inlet valves by pushrods and rockers, the other working the side exhausts. The inlet valves were of Mercedes' own 'annular' type, having a series of apertures in the head which admitted extra gas on opening.

The crankshaft ran in three broad main bearings, the massive cylinders were cast in two blocks of two, and a Mercedes spiral spring scroll-type clutch transmitted the power via a cardan shaft to a big separate four-speed gearbox and countershafts carrying the sprockets for the chain final drive. To achieve a lower chassis line, the front dumb-irons curved upwards over the elegantly formed axle, while for the first time the body-work curved round the scuttle to give driver and mechanic some protection. Although these great white cars represented the 'monsters' of the heroic racing age at their peak, and were built to Teutonic standards of strength and efficiency, they were far from

A classic from 'the age of monsters', the 12·8-litre Mercedes with which Lautenschlager won the 1908 Grand Prix at Dieppe at 69·05mph. Another Mercedes finished fifth, while the third team car set the fastest lap of the race at 78·89mph

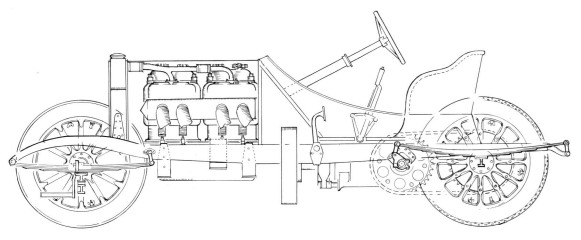

heavy, scaling 2464lb on the Dieppe weighbridge – substantially lighter than all other competitors save the French Porthos, which were not serious rivals.

Their appearance was superbly balanced, with the radiator set well back behind the front-wheel centre line, a neat rear fuel tank, and four extremely impressive exhaust pipes sprouting from the bonnet on the left-hand side and terminating in a tailpipe like a drain. In the Grand Prix they exceeded 100mph at some points, and with poor road surfaces made poorer by an earlier voiturette race, tyre trouble was rampant. Covers disintegrated under the pace and weight, making speedy tyre changing vital; with typical foresight, the Mercedes team had the advantage, not only of a new type Michelin one-bolt quickly-detachable wheel rim, but also of special pneumatic jacks.

On the very first lap Salzer in one Mercedes set the fastest lap at 78·89mph to draw the opposition, though he paid for it with swift retirement. Then Lautenschlager, driving his very first race, took the lead on lap five. During a pitiless race lasting close on seven hours he used up 11 tyres and had to nurse the Mercedes through the corners to save precious rubber over the last 96 miles, no more tyres being available. Watched by Paul Daimler he won at 69·05mph by nearly nine minutes from two compatriot Benz – a truly crushing defeat for the proud French.

The demise of the Grand Prix until 1912 denied the 135hp Mercedes further opportunity to race in Europe, other than in Continental hillclimbs and sprints, and short Brooklands races. Two cars went to the United States, however, Ralph de Palma winning both the Vanderbilt Cup and Elgin Trophy road races in 1912. The de Palma car was fitted with a later Mercedes engine, the 9·6-litre 37/90 type, and it also contested that year's Indianapolis 500 Miles race. The big, grey-painted Mercedes led from the start, but with a mere two laps to go, when 10 miles ahead of the second car, it broke a piston. The driver and mechanic pushed it a full two miles to the finishing line, but for all their valiant efforts were unplaced.

Specification

Engine
Four cylinders, in-line; bore and stroke, 154·7 × 170mm; capacity, 12781cc. Pushrod-operated overhead inlet valves, side exhaust valves, two per cylinder; single Mercedes carburetter; Bosch h-t magneto; maximum power, 135bhp at 1400rpm.

Transmission
Separate four-speed gearbox, chain final drive.

Chassis
Pressed channel-section side members; semi-elliptic springing front and rear; Mercedes drum-type friction dampers. Internal expanding rear-wheel brakes and transmission brake. Michelin detachable rims and tyres.

Dimensions
Wheelbase, 8ft 10in; track, 4ft 7·5in; dry weight, 2464lb.

Maximum speed
104mph.

1912 Grand Prix Peugeot L76

'I had a fine car, with a wonderfully efficient engine, for with only 110 mm bore it could more than hold its own with engines of 155 mm bore...'

Georges Boillot

Opposite, top: the great innovation on the 1912 Grand Prix Peugeot engine was the use of 16 valves and twin overhead camshafts, setting a pattern which still prevails today. On this early interpretation the camshafts were driven by a vertical shaft, bevels and pinions, while the stems and springs of the inclined valves were exposed. Through more efficient breathing and burning, and increased rpm, this engine improved on the performance of earlier engines of twice its size

Opposite, bottom: a light-alloy differential housing helped keep the weight of the GP Peugeot rear axle below 225lb. Suspension was by semi-elliptic leaf springs, checked by friction shock absorbers and leather rebound straps. Large-diameter internal expanding brakes featured, while the cylindrical fuel tank was obligatory under the ACF rules

Peugeot's first Grand Prix car made international impact when, in the year following its 1912 victory at Dieppe, it won America's greatest race, the Indianapolis 500. Here is winner Jules Goux, whose 76·59 mph average took him over 13 minutes ahead of two American cars by the finish. His car was lined down from 7·6 to 7·4 litres (450cu in) to comply with race rules

For four long years the French had to endure the humiliation of their double defeat in the Grand Prix – by Fiat in 1907 and Mercedes in 1908. The major manufacturers had agreed that racing was too expensive, and the ACF's great event was not revived until 1912, by which time a formidable new French marque had come to the forefront. Peugeot, a very old name associated with textiles, tools, coffee mills, spectacles, crinolines, bicycles and many other things, began making cars in 1889. They took up voiturette racing and did well up to 1911, when the GP de la Sarthe for cars limited to 110mm bore × 200mm stroke four-cylinder engines was announced at Le Mans. The stalwarts of the Peugeot team, Georges Boillot, Jules Goux and Paul Zuccarelli, persuaded Robert Peugeot to back the construction of advanced new cars at Beaulieu-Valentigney for this race. They were not completed in time, but the 'three Charlatans' as the trio were called, found a welcome new target in the revived French Grand Prix, due to be run at Dieppe in July 1912.

Chief draughtsman on the L76 project was a 26-year-old Swiss named Ernest Henry, whose main function, it is believed, was to transpose the Charlatans' thoughts on to the drawing board. However, the 1912 Peugeot engine is often attributed to him, it being as difficult then to apportion credit fairly as it is on today's Formula 1 cars. Primary inspiration for the overall Peugeot design is thought to have come from Zuccarelli, a fine engineer/driver formerly with the Spanish Hispano-Suiza company, but whoever the design kingpin, the product became historic

as the 'giant killer' which ended the 'age of monsters' by the scientific approach.

Even the chain-drive 'monsters', as exemplified by the S74 Fiat, had acquired an overhead camshaft by 1912, but Peugeot went further by having *two*, which operated two inlet and two exhaust valves per cylinder, set at 45 degrees in the head. According to one French source, this was not the very first twin overhead camshaft engine, Delahaye making one in 1907, believedly for a boat, although Peugeot first saw its value for motor racing. Advantages included a compact hemispherical-shaped combustion chamber able to accommodate four valves, crossflow porting, central sparking plug location, and less reciprocating weight. An unusual method of ensuring positive valve actuation was the use of bronze 'D' or stirrup-shaped tappets surrounding each cam, which both opened and closed the valves with assistance from light springs – an early form of desmodromic operation which Peugeot dropped a year later. Zuccarelli and Henry also exploited valve overlap between the opening of the inlets and the closing of the exhausts to improve breathing and combustion.

The integral iron head and block, cast as a monobloc, measured 110 × 200mm (7598cc) and produced 130bhp at 2250rpm, compared with the bigger Fiat's 140bhp at 1600rpm from almost twice the capacity. The crankshaft ran in five plain whitemetal main bearings in an alloy crankcase, the camshafts being driven via bevels, a vertical shaft and pinions. Pistons, connecting rods and crankshaft were made from special Derihon BND high-tensile steel; wet sump high-pressure lubrication was employed, ignition was by Bosch high-tension magneto and carburation by a single Claudel. The drive passed through a multi-plate clutch, separate four-speed gearbox and open propellor 'Hotchkiss' drive, wherein the rear semi-elliptic springs absorbed axle torque. Setting a new Grand Prix fashion, the wheels were of Rudge-Whitworth detachable wire type retained by ring nuts; a year later ears were added and the 'knock-off' cap was born.

The car won back the coveted Grand Prix for France first time out in 1912, although Georges Boillot was lucky to win. The ACF had reverted to the unpopular two-day race over 956 exhausting miles of the 47·8-mile Dieppe circuit, and the distance was very nearly Peugeot's undoing. Boillot was runner-up to one of the big single-cam Fiats on the first day, and in the second half a stirring Fiat-Peugeot duel ended when the

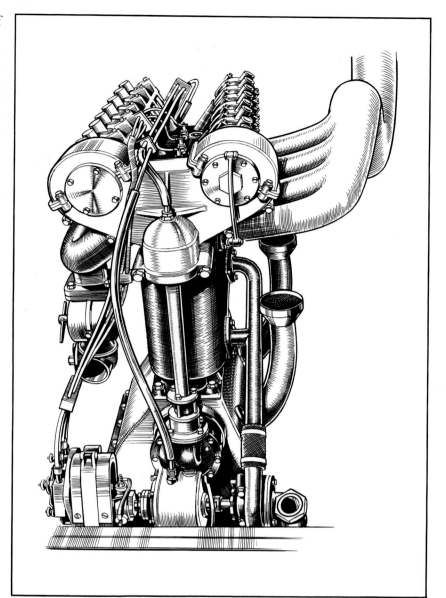

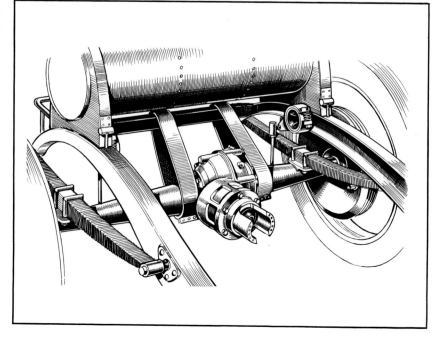

*Ending 'the age of
monsters', Georges Boillot's
7·6-litre Peugeot L76
winning the 956-mile,
two-day French Grand Prix
at Dieppe in 1912*

Italian car broke a petrol pipe. Dogged by a second Fiat, the Peugeot itself ran into trouble, losing first and third gears. Boillot finally nursed it home to win at 68·45 mph.

Then the dashing Georges broke the Mont Ventoux mountain record, while Goux won the 401-mile Sarthe Cup race at Le Mans. In 1913 Goux brought a special streamlined, track-bodied version of the L76 to England, scoring a first and a second at the Brooklands Easter meeting and then breaking several world records including the Hour, which he and Boillot raised to 106·22 mph.

Two Peugeots in GP form then crossed the Atlantic for the 1913 Indianapolis 500 Miles Race. To meet the 450 cu in (7·4-litre) limit they were reduced to 113 × 184 mm bore and stroke (capacity 7384 cc), and Goux outpaced all American opposition to win the race and $20000 in prize money. The high-speed, high-efficiency engine had arrived in two Continents, and soon twin overhead camshafts were an essential layout for Grand Prix winners, as indeed they still are today.

Specification
Engine
Four cylinders, in-line; bore and stroke, 110 × 200 mm; capacity 7598 cc; twin overhead camshafts operating four valves per cylinder; single Claudel carburetter; Bosch h-t magneto; maximum power, 130 bhp at 2250 rpm.
Transmission
Separate four-speed gearbox, propellor-shaft final drive.
Chassis
Pressed-steel side members; semi-elliptic leaf springing front and rear; Hartford drum-type friction dampers. Internal expanding rear brakes and transmission brake. Continental tyres.
Dimensions
Wheelbase, 9ft 1in; track, 4ft 6in front and rear; dry weight, 1974 lb.
Maximum speed
102 mph.

1914 Mercedes

'His Majesty the Kaiser is delighted at the fine success of the Mercedes cars and drivers and sends his congratulations.'

Telegram received by Mercedes, 1914

Good ideas seldom catch on at once. Although the twin overhead camshaft 16-valve Peugeot pointed the way in 1912 and 1913, not every designer rushed to copy it. Certainly three prominent rivals did so for the 1914 Grand Prix, but more opted for the simpler single camshaft, the most notable dissidents being Mercedes of Germany who, as befitted the pioneer firm from Unterturkheim, followed no fashion but did things their own way. Their last ACF Grand Prix was that of 1908, which they won, after which they became much preoccupied with aircraft engines, picking up invaluable experience in light cylinder construction and other weight-saving factors. All this helped when they decided to contest the 1914 Grand Prix at Lyon with five cars at the thumping entrance fee of 3000 gold francs each.

With typical Swabian caution and thoroughness they had made a 'dummy run' with a variety of designs in the 1913 GP de la Sarthe at Le Mans, scoring a modest third and convincing themselves that six cylinders were not necessary, that high-revving engines were, and that shaft final drive was better than chains. Their preparation for the race at Lyon in July 1914 was extremely painstaking. While the Daimler aero-engine section were building the new GP engines, limited to $4\frac{1}{2}$ litres, drivers and technicians 'recce'd' the 23·3-mile road circuit in touring cars. They documented every straight and turn, every gradient, bump, hollow and camber, checked fuel consumption and tyre behaviour, and practised assiduously day after day. They then returned to Germany and built all the desired factors into their five racing cars.

Designed by Paul Daimler, Fritz Nallinger Sr and others, the superb 1914 GP Mercedes had a 93 × 165mm, 4483cc engine which embodied aero engine practice in having four separate machined steel cylinders with integral four-valve heads, welded-on valve

'Mercedes über alles' was uncomfortably emphasised to the French at their 1914 Grand Prix on the Lyon circuit, when three of these elegant white cars stormed home in the first three places. The $4\frac{1}{2}$-litre four-cylinder overhead camshaft engine drove through a separate four-speed gearbox; the vee radiator, enclosed cockpit and full-length undershield all contributed to reduce drag, and 115bhp produced close on 115mph

18 years' development of the Grand Prix shape: Above: the 1906 Renault offered sparse protection for its occupants, with the whole cockpit area wide open to the elements

Below: creature comforts and 'windcutting' needs get more consideration on the 1908 GP-winning Mercedes with some cowling and side protection; the front splash guards were road wear when driving from factory to circuit and back

Opposite, top: an incipient tail and full-length undershield emphasise the growing awareness of the drag factor on the 1914 Mercedes, again equipped for road use

Opposite, lower: the 1924 Type 35 Bugatti looks superbly 'right' with its small frontal area and efficient body shape with wedge tail

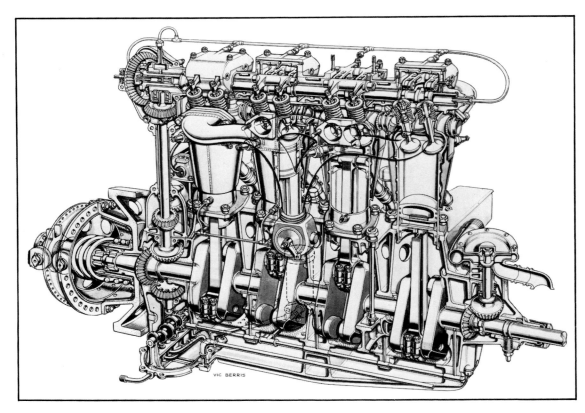

ports and water jackets, aluminium crank-case and single shaft-driven overhead cam-shaft. The valves were inclined at 60 degrees and operated by rockers; there were three plugs to each cylinder, twin Bosch magnetos, a single Mercedes updraught carburetter, and wet-sump full-pressure lubrication with individual feed pipes to vital bearings, echo-ing aviation practice in its thoroughness. After test breakages, the five-bearing crank-shafts were remade in Austrian 'Aquila' steel and meticulously counter-balanced, while special Eisemann plugs with platinum points had to be made to withstand revolutions of over 3000rpm.

The chassis embodied a central X-bracing and semi-elliptic springs all round, and trans-mission was by double cone clutch, separate four-speed gearbox, propellor shaft and torque tube to a live rear axle. This embodied twin driving pinions with the differential in between and a crownwheel to each half-shaft, a system reducing wheelspin and allowing positive camber of the rear wheels. Rudge-Whitworth wire wheels with knock-off caps carried Continental tyres, each wheel being carefully balanced – a further innovation in motor racing. The body was strikingly Teu-tonic with its deep vee radiator and crisply chiselled lines, ending in an incipient tail enclosing the spare wheels. At last the 'sit up and beg' seating of the 'monster age' had gone, and the driver and mechanic sat *in*, rather than *on* their car, with benefits in

reduced drag. The Mercedes crews also enjoyed the unusual luxury of a bottle of cold drink in the cockpit, with a rubber pipe for imbibing – an early anticipation of Louis Chiron's famous champagne flask!

DMG's engine gave 115bhp at 3200rpm, and an unladen weight of 2380lb (the ACF maximum limit was 2419lb) meant a maxi-mum speed close to 115mph. Toughest opposition amongst the 37 entries undoubt-edly came from the three 4½-litre twin-cam four-wheel braked Peugeots, headed by the tempestuous Georges Boillot. The legend has flourished that Mercedes conducted their 1914 Grand Prix like a military operation, with the pits ordering cars forward like chess-pieces, but in truth there was no rigid control. Test engineer and team manager Dipl Ing Alfred Vischer simply instructed his drivers to try to hold the leaders and stop at half-distance for tyres and further instructions according to the situation. Indeed, there was considerable rivalry between the 'old guard' drivers Lautenschlager and Salzer, and the 'new boy' Max Sailer, and a modicum of 'we told you so' satisfaction when the latter's car broke at least one connecting rod on lap five after leading the race and making fastest lap at 69·65mph. With stricter pit control Sailer would not have pressed so hard, al-though by involuntarily playing the hare he probably caused Boillot to overstress his Peugeot.

Lautenschlager, the 1908 winner, dogged

the Frenchman relentlessly and caught him on lap 18 to win his second Grand Prix, while the Peugeot wilted and broke down with one lap to go, whereupon the Mercedes of Wagner and Salzer swept by to complete a devastating one-two-three victory by the Germans. Goux's surviving Peugeot was fourth, over nine minutes behind Lautenschlager, who averaged 65·66mph for the 467·7 miles of this unforgettable Grand Prix. Since a major objective of racing was to advertise one's products, it was ironic that a potential Mercedes sales boom should be sabotaged four weeks later when Kaiser Wilhelm II precipitated the First World War. Fortunately the American driver Ralph de Palma managed to ship one of the cars out to the States, where he won the 1914 Elgin road race, 1915 Indianapolis 500 Miles and numerous lesser events. After the war another Lyon Mercedes went to Italy, where Count Giulio Masetti won the 'Gentlemen's Amateur GP' at Brescia in 1921 and the 1922 Targa Florio, for which gruelling race it was equipped with four-wheel brakes.

Specification

Engine
Four cylinders, in-line; bore and stroke, 93 × 165mm; capacity, 4483cc; single overhead camshaft operating four valves per cylinder; single Mercedes carburetter; twin Bosch h-t magnetos; three plugs per cylinder; maximum power, 115bhp at 3200rpm.

Transmission
Separate four-speed gearbox, torque-tube final drive.

Chassis
Pressed-steel side members; semi-elliptic leaf springs front and rear; duplicated Mercedes face-cam dampers. Internal expanding rear-wheel brakes and transmission brake. Continental tyres.

Dimensions
Wheelbase, 9ft 4in; front track, 4ft 4·5in; rear track, 4ft 5in; dry weight, 2380lb.

Maximum speed
115mph.

The purposeful, almost menacing shape of the 1914 Mercedes, with its clean, low build and huge outside exhaust pipe is emphasised in this shot of Christian Lautenschlager forcing on to victory

Louis Wagner, second man home at Lyon, in his Mercedes. Note the prominent vee radiator, the severe, 'chiselled' lines behind it, the unusual crossed straps, untidy fuel piping outside the rear tank, and the absence of front-wheel brakes

Opposite, top: *double fame: renowned for its voiturette racing feats in 1936, the ex-Richard Seaman 1½-litre straight-eight Delage, as restored by present owner R. R. C. Walker, was itself descended from the remarkable 1926–27 Grand Prix Delage with which Benoist won four Grands Prix in 1927 (see page 42)*

Opposite, lower: *out of failure, success: A surviving example of the 1922 2-litre four-cylinder Sunbeam, which was outpaced in the Grand Prix at Strasbourg by the Fiats. From it sprang the successful 1923 and 1924 Grand Prix Sunbeam sixes (see page 32)*

A famous American: Leon Duray's front-drive 1½-litre eight-cylinder Miller '91' (see page 45), one of two which he brought to Europe to race, and eventually to dispose of, in 1929. The cars were rediscovered at Bugatti's Molsheim factory many years later, returned to the USA in 1959, and restored to exhibition standards

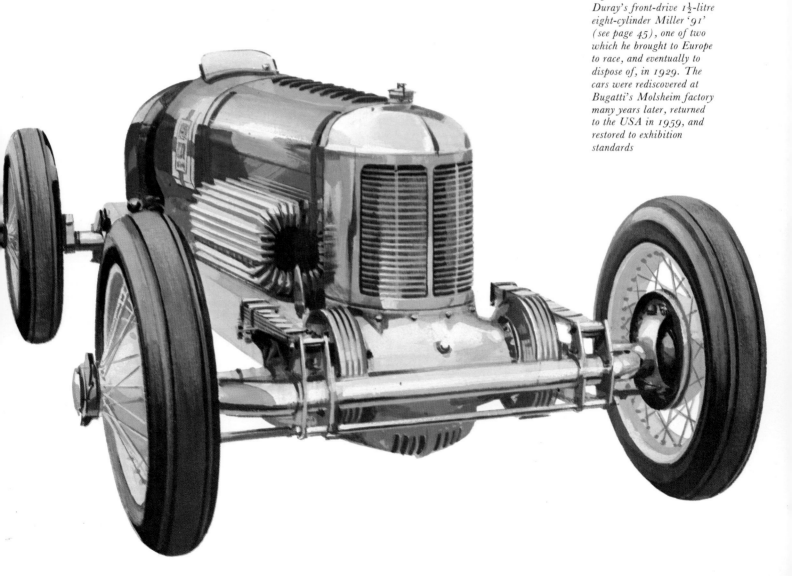

1921 Grand Prix Duesenberg

'The Yankees gained yards going into the corners—and coming out of them. We were in another race!'

K. Lee Guinness, Talbot driver

'The American team, accustomed to tracks, will find themselves handicapped on the road. I foresee victory going to Ballot.' Thus Maurice Philippe in *Automobilia* on prospects for the first post-war French Grand Prix, held at Le Mans on July 25th, 1921. His words echoed French feelings as a whole, and their acute disappointment when three sleek white and blue Duesenbergs from the USA finished one-four-six recalled an infinitely darker July day in 1914, when a more sinister breed of foreign white cars had routed the French.

It was a common error then to assume that the Americans only raced on tracks like Indianapolis, Uniontown, Tacoma, Beverly Hills and Los Angeles, at all of which the straight-eight Duesenbergs from New Jersey had shone. The French should have recalled another American event at Elgin, Illinois, won in 1920 by one of their own 3-litre Ballots driven by masterly Ralph de Palma. This was no top gear track race; the 250-mile Elgin National was held regularly over a rough and tricky 8·5-mile road circuit, and Etablissements Ballot of Malakoff, Paris, deemed it important enough to send their engineer Jean Marcenac over specially to fit a set of servo-operated front brakes to de Palma's car. These enabled him to beat the Duesenberg, Monroe and Frontenac opposition by over a minute, and although the

'Power of the hour' was the Duesenberg engine manufacturing company's slogan, highly appropriate to the 3-litre straight-eight unit which propelled their cars to 1st, 4th and 6th places in the 1921 French Grand Prix at Le Mans. A single shaft-driven overhead camshaft operated two exhaust and one inlet valve per cylinder, tubular connecting rods featured, and the engine gave 114bhp at 4250rpm with excellent torque

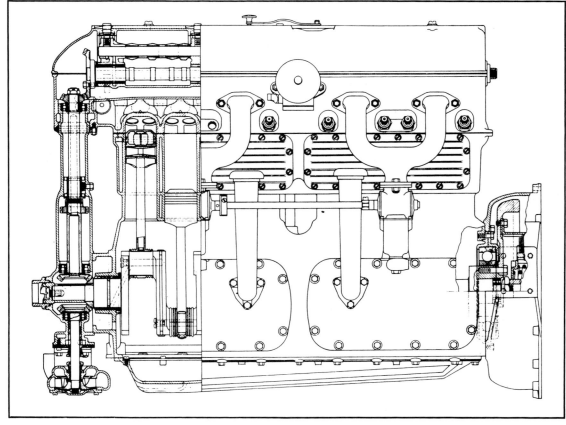

'Dueseys' that finished two-three-five also had four-wheel brakes these had not proved effective. In this factor lay the seeds of France's 1921 Grand Prix defeat. . . .

The French marque naturally entered a full team, but Duesenberg's surprise four-car entry came in late, and the ACF's exorbitant excess fees at about £1200 per car (with not a *sou* in prize money!) were paid by French expatriate Albert Champion, US sparking plug tycoon. Apart from both being 3-litre straight eights, the rival cars differed widely. The Ballots followed Peugeot style with twin overhead camshafts and four valves per cylinder whereas Duesenberg employed a single overhead camshaft operating two exhaust valves and one big inlet valve per cylinder. They also had three-bearing crank-shafts to Ballot's five, three-speed gearboxes in unit with the engine (the French cars had separate four-speed boxes) and Delco coil-and-battery ignition instead of magnetos, a result of Delco's generous bonuses to users at Indianapolis. Ballot's declared output was 107bhp at 3800rpm to Duesenberg's 114bhp at 4250rpm, which the French unwisely dismissed as American boasting.

There was one other difference. Profiting from their Elgin defeat, the brothers Fred and August Duesenberg scrapped the cable actuation of their four-wheel brakes and adopted a new hydraulic system developed by Scots-born Malcolm Loughead, a California-based engineer who later spelt his name Lockheed and gained world fame. On the GP Duesenberg, the hydraulic fluid (a mixture of glycerine and water rather than today's oil) passed from the master cylinder through flexible piping into the tubular axle ends, then through holes in the kingpin centres to bronze pistons in vertical cylinders which expanded the shoes through toggles. For oil tightness they relied on precision-ground fitting throughout, but fluid loss was also offset by a reserve tank connected by a valve to the master cylinder.

At weighing-in the lightest Duesenberg scaled 910kg to the best Ballot's 932kg, thanks to lighter transmission, single shock absorbers instead of double, and the absence of spare wheels. In practice *les Yankees* quickly upset the French by equalling the Ballots' times, for to offset their three-speed gearboxes, their 'torquey' engines picking up crisply to a rasping 5000rpm, while deceleration was equally impressive. In one case it was *too* good, a locked front brake overturning Jimmy Murphy's car and casting out both him and his passenger, Duesenberg's number four driver Louis Inghibert. Murphy sustained badly bruised ribs requiring heavy bandaging for the race, but Inghibert had to be replaced by André Dubonnet.

Two of the sleek white and blue Duesenbergs spread themselves at the pits, while Segrave in his Talbot pulls out with much gesticulation. No. 12 is Jimmy Murphy's winning car, his mechanic changing a rear wheel

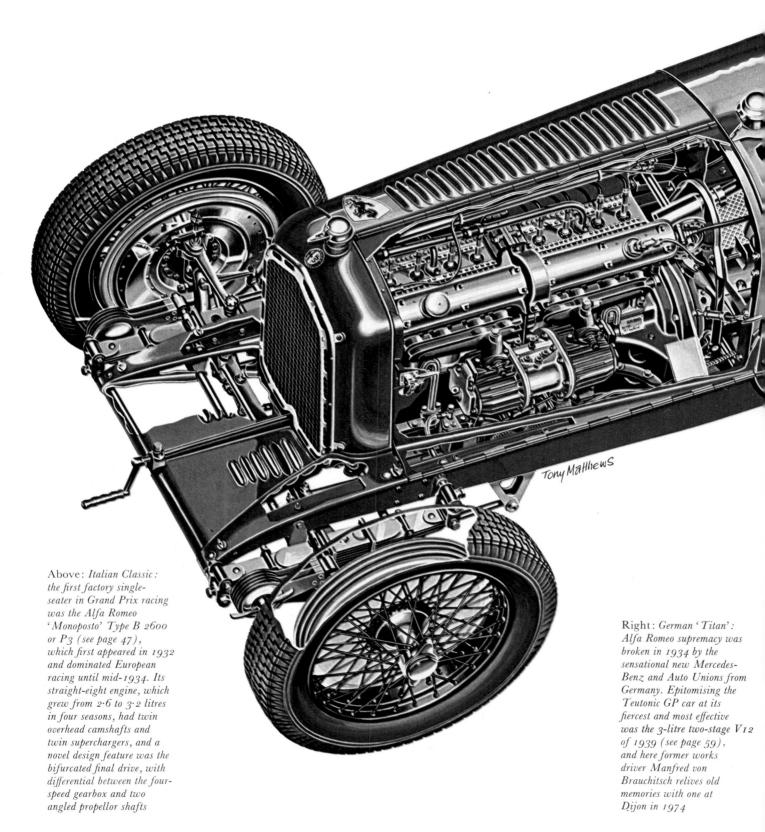

Tony Matthews

Above: *Italian Classic: the first factory single-seater in Grand Prix racing was the Alfa Romeo 'Monoposto' Type B 2600 or P3 (see page 47), which first appeared in 1932 and dominated European racing until mid-1934. Its straight-eight engine, which grew from 2·6 to 3·2 litres in four seasons, had twin overhead camshafts and twin superchargers, and a novel design feature was the bifurcated final drive, with differential between the four-speed gearbox and two angled propellor shafts*

Right: *German 'Titan': Alfa Romeo supremacy was broken in 1934 by the sensational new Mercedes-Benz and Auto Unions from Germany. Epitomising the Teutonic GP car at its fiercest and most effective was the 3-litre two-stage V12 of 1939 (see page 59), and here former works driver Manfred von Brauchitsch relives old memories with one at Dijon in 1974*

The Grand Prix Duesenberg and blackened crew, seen just after winning. The right-hand rear tyre is flat, and one front tyre looks that way too, eloquent of the harsh circuit conditions

The race quickly devolved into a Ballot-Duesenberg battle, while the circuit rapidly broke up as pounding wheels kicked up large flints and hurled them around like deadly shrapnel. On lap 12 leader Murphy had to stop to change two tyres, letting Chassagne's Ballot through, but six laps later the French car's fuel tank collapsed on to the propellor shaft. Boyer then led until a stone smashed into his radiator, the engine seized and a con rod broke. With two rounds to go a sharp flint pierced Murphy's radiator too, while another punctured a tyre. He hobbled to the pits for a new wheel and water, not daring to switch his overheated engine off, and finally the American nursed the hot, smoking, Duesenberg to a sensational victory.

Greatly helped by his front brakes, Murphy averaged 78·1mph for 321·68 miles of atrocious roads, also making fastest lap at 83·40mph, a speed unequalled at Le Mans until 1930 despite cars such as 6½-litre Bentleys contesting the subsequent 24 Hours race there on infinitely better road surfaces. Back in the USA the beautiful Duesenbergs won six more races that season, two at Cotati and others at Uniontown, Beverly Hills, Santa Rosa and San Carlos, where Murphy rounded off 1921 with a sizzling 111·8mph win in the 250-mile race. His $1000 first

prize was $1000 more than he earned at Le Mans, although it is for their great victory there that he and the handsome 183cu in Duesenberg will always be remembered internationally.

Specification
Engine
Eight cylinders; in-line; bore and stroke, 63·5 × 117mm; capacity, 2977cc; single overhead camshaft operating three valves per cylinder; two Miller carburetters on winning car, two Claudels on others; Delco coil and distributor ignition; maximum power, 114bhp at 4250rpm.
Transmission
Three-speed gearbox in unit with engine, torque-tube final drive.
Chassis
Pressed-steel side members; semi-elliptic springing front and rear; single Monroe friction dampers front and rear. Four-wheel hydraulic brakes. Firestone Oldfield tyres.
Dimensions
Wheelbase, 8ft 9·5in; track, 4ft 3in front and rear; dry weight, 2002lb.
Maximum speed
112mph.

1922
2-litre Fiat

'It was Italy's triumph, complete, decisive, incontestable. The French seemed displeased.'

'Auto-Moto-Ciclo'

Considering the popularity of straight eights in racing since 1919, it was surprising that the most successful 1922 car, the Type 804 Fiat, had six cylinders. Expediency was the reason. Fiat valued the in-line eight layout as much as anyone for its virtues of high power, low stress and flexibility, and had built their own in 1921 – an advanced 65 × 112mm twin-cam unit departing from current convention in having only two valves per cylinder and a crankshaft running in split roller main and big-end bearings rather than plain white metal. These permitted it 4600rpm to the Duesenberg's 4250rpm and the Ballot's 3800rpm, but serious labour troubles in Italy so delayed its completion that it missed the 1921 French GP and only just made the first Italian GP at Brescia. It showed its potential there by leading the Ballots over half way and setting the fastest lap before trouble set in, but with a new 2-litre Formula imminent for 1922–25, this promising car all too soon became redundant.

It earned its keep, however, by providing the basis for two outstanding smaller Fiats, a four-cylinder 1½-litre voiturette which used literally one half of the engine, and the 1922 2-litre Type 804. Chief designer Giulio Cappa regarded the latter as a 'stop gap', the 3-litre's stroke being reduced to 100mm and

the cylinders to six, in two blocks of three. The resultant 1991cc unit set new fashions in GP design which instantly outmoded the 'Henry school'. Like its 3-litre forebear, the engine had cylinders and water jackets built up by welding, a process used on Fiat's wartime aero-engines but originally 'borrowed' from Mercedes, sabotaging the haughty claim that 'Fiat does not copy, it teaches'. But in other aspects Turin certainly taught its rivals; its one-piece counter-balanced crankshaft ran in seven split roller bearing mains, enabling it to rotate at over 5000rpm, the big ends also had roller bearings, and dry sump lubrication lowered the engine line.

Chrome-nickel connecting rods carried domed aluminium pistons, as essential by 1922 as twin overhead camshafts and four-wheel brakes. But Fiat chose two large valves per cylinder at 96 degrees instead of the fashionable four, while the four-speed gearbox was in unit with the engine, a Fiat feature since 1914. The low, semi-elliptically sprung chassis had notably slender side members and front springs which passed through forged slots in the tubular front axle, a design sophistication first practised on the 1914 GP Vauxhall. From front to rear the chassis and body followed the same elegant and effective 'tear drop' contours, tapering in to the flat-sided

Following pages: Two ages of Alfa: a 1951 1½-litre Type 159 Alfa Romeo of the type with which Fangio won his first World Championship heads an older brother, a 1932 2·6-litre P3 'Monoposto', off the line at Dijon in the 1974 'Retrospective' demonstration of past Grand Prix winners

Star of Strasbourg in 1922 was undoubtedly Fiat's new 2-litre six-cylinder Type 804; it set the pace and decimated the opposition, only dire misfortune through a flaw in the rear axle denying the Italian marque a 1–2–3 triumph

'wedge' tail adopted by Fiat in 1919, the entire design being evolved with help from Fiat aerodynamicist Rosatelli and his department's wind tunnel.

Seldom was the tenet 'if it looks right it is right' better upheld. The Fiat 804 was small, with an 8ft 2½in wheelbase, light at 1500lb unladen, extremely accelerative and, when its 94bhp at 5200rpm was fully extended, capable of about 104mph in Strasbourg form. In extracting the optimum, the Turin engineers perhaps cut too closely into safety margins, for their triumphant one-two-three formation in the 499-mile French GP was brutally shattered during the last nine laps. Destructive vibration fractured a flange on the rear axle housing, which was ingeniously fabricated from welded steel pressings rather than cast, resulting in lost wheels on two cars, and one driver's life. The remaining 804, driven by veteran Nazzaro, went on to win by almost an hour over two Bugattis.

It was a harsh lesson in the hazards of metal fatigue, and after this *vittoria dolorosa* Fiat prepared for September's Italian GP on the new Monza speedway. They modified the axle housings and raised engine output to 112 bhp at 5200 rpm, quite needlessly as it proved. Their overwhelming superiority at Strasbourg had a drastic 'Big Jake's a'coming' effect on the Italian GP, an imposing 39-car entry on paper becoming a modest eight on the grid for the first massed start in GP racing. The sleek red Fiats just galloped off with the 497-mile race, Bordino the victor at 86·8mph from Nazzaro, with a Bugatti nine laps in arrears.

Back in 1907 Nazzaro and Fiat had won the French GP at 70·61mph on 16·3 litres and 130bhp. In 1922 the same pairing won the same race at 79·33mph on 2 litres and 94bhp,

a lesson in the potential of the small, high-efficiency engine, yet due for sensational eclipse within a year. Fiat had their 2-litre straight eights ready for 1923, fitting them into slightly lengthened 804 chassis carrying even sleeker bodywork. This new Type 805 brought supercharging to GP racing, first using a German-patented eccentric vane blower which cost Fiat the 1923 French GP through inadequate intake filtering. Replacement by a Roots-type 'figure-of-eight' supercharger produced a 130bhp racing car which scored a second sweeping one-two victory at Monza at 91·06mph, with fastest lap at 98·6mph, a devastating testimony to Fiat 'teaching' precipitating a cult for forced induction destined to last nearly 30 years.

Specification
Engine
Six cylinders, in-line; bore and stroke, 65 × 100mm; capacity, 1991cc; twin overhead camshafts operating two valves per cylinder; single Fiat carburetter; Marelli h-t magneto; maximum power, 94bhp at 5200rpm, rising to 112bhp at 5200rpm.
Transmission
Four-speed gearbox in unit with engine; torque-tube final drive.
Chassis
Pressed-steel side members; semi-elliptic springing front and rear; Hartford friction dampers. Four-wheel internal expanding brakes. Pirelli tyres.
Dimensions
Wheelbase, 8ft 2·5in; track, 3ft 11·5in front and rear, dry weight, 1502lb.
Maximum speed
104mph.

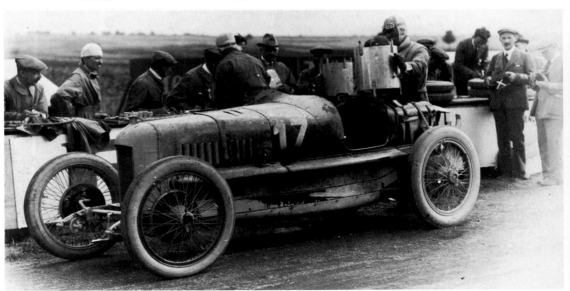

2-litre Grand Prix Sunbeam

'There were special reasons why the Sunbeams should have six, and not four, eight or twelve cylinders.'

'The Autocar', 1923

The law of evolution applies to racing cars as much as to other things, and a principle, once proven, is inevitably followed. Louis Coatalen, Breton-born chief designer of the Sunbeam Motor Company of Wolverhampton, has frequently been accused of interpreting this law too literally by simply copying good designs, such as the 1913 twin overhead camshaft Peugeot which inspired his 1914 TT and GP Sunbeams, and the 1922 Fiat Type 804, the basic concept of which can clearly be seen in the 1923 GP Sunbeam. What Coatalen did, in fact, in the latter case, was to *hire* the Italian Vincenzo Bertarione and his aide, Walter Becchia, who had both worked with the Fornaca-Cappa-Cavalli team on the 1922 Fiat, to design a new Sunbeam for 1923; whether Coatalen expressly bade his new employees to copy the Fiat, or whether Bertarione did it of his own volition is not known. Ironically, Fiat's six was a transitional design pending fruition of their more advanced, supercharged straight eight, yet the British-built 'Fiats in green paint' won the race!

Although Sunbeam's earlier long-stroke 16-valve four-cylinder cars had failed in the 1922 Grands Prix, Bertarione and Becchia employed a similar chassis with the same built-up front axle, Hotchkiss-type final drive and servo brakes for 1923, designing it to fit their new Fiat-inspired six-cylinder 12-valve engine. As a token of originality this measured 67×94mm to the Fiat's 65×100mm, the cylinders, in two blocks of three, being of forged steel with welded sheet steel water jackets, all following Turin's lead. A Solex rather than a Fiat carburetter, but on a very similar manifold, and Bosch magneto instead of a Marelli, were face-saving variations, and whereas Fiat claimed 112bhp for their 804 in Monza form, Sunbeam more modestly cited 108bhp at 5000rpm. Yet crankshaft speeds of up to 6000rpm were quoted by Coatalen, made feasible by eight roller main bearings, roller big ends and high pressure dry sump lubrication.

Sunbeams were said to have encountered considerable difficulty building these engines, but the cars performed satisfactorily in

British victory: Henry O'Neal de Hane Segrave in the Wolverhampton-built 2-litre unsupercharged six-cylinder Sunbeam with which he won the 1923 French Grand Prix on the Tours circuit

Out in front: Segrave in the supercharged Sunbeam completing the second lap of the 1924 Grand Prix at Lyon, well ahead of the opposition. Persistent misfiring set in after lap 3, and although he made the record lap Segrave could only finish a disappointed 5th

early tests at Brooklands, after which they were *driven* from Wolverhampton to Tours, scene of the Grand Prix, emphasising the tractability of Grand Prix racing cars – and of road laws! – over 50 years ago. Italy's fierce, supercharged eight-cylinder Fiats set the pace in the race, only to drop out one by one as their unscreened superchargers choked on the dust of the cars they lapped. Then the Sunbeams, fastest among the rest despite diverse troubles, moved up, Segrave passing the last sick Fiat with two laps to go, and scoring the first British victory ever in a Grand Prix, his team mates completing the triumph for racing green by taking second and fourth places.

Although Coatalen shied from facing the blown Fiats a second time in the Italian GP, he sent two cars to the new Sitges speedway for the Spanish GP meeting in October. They met worthy opposition from Zborowski's fast, single-seater, straight eight Miller, which was leading two laps from the finish when a tyre burst, letting Divo's Sunbeam through to win the 248·5-mile race, while the other Sunbeam retired. But if Sunbeam won races in 1923 when they didn't deserve to, Fate squared the account in 1924.

Wolverhampton again followed Turin's road by adopting supercharging for 1924, but they showed praiseworthy originality in their approach to the problem. Using a Roots-type blower, chief engineer J. S. Irving tried the Italian method of compressing air through the carburetter, and then reversed the order, fitting the carburetter outside the blower and compressing mixture into the engine. It worked well, Irving getting a brake reading of 138 bhp at 5500 rpm, a gain of 36 horsepower over the 1923 engine, with added power advantage at lower engine speeds.

Sunbeams were the first European makers to adopt this arrangement, and proved the fastest cars in the 1924 Grand Prix at Lyon.

To accommodate the new supercharged engines, the 1923 cars were considerably rebuilt, the chassis being 4 in longer and the track widened. A new, four-speed gearbox with central gearchange and torque tube final drive featured, and lower, sleeker but larger bodies were built, the supercharging compensating for an increase of nearly 280 lb in weight. In the race, Segrave took an immediate lead over the rival Fiats, Alfa Romeos and Delages, but pulled in for plugs

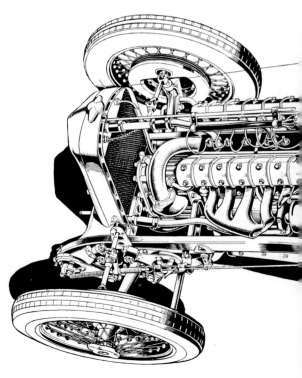

on lap three and was plagued with misfiring to the end of the 503-mile race, finishing a frustrated fifth, but with the record lap to his credit. K.Lee Guinness in the second car took the lead on lap 16, then burst a tyre and finally broke a transmission joint, while Resta's car suffered the same misfiring as Segrave's and was flagged off.

After the race the misfiring was traced to defective magnetos fitted new shortly before the race as a precaution. When one of the old 1923 instruments was refitted all misfiring vanished. Some recompense came in the subsequent GP at San Sebastian, Spain, where Segrave won after a masterly drive. It was the last *grande epreuve* victory by a British car for no less than 33 years, when Vanwall broke the long, long drought. Sunbeam's racing efforts gradually petered out after 1924. Count Masetti drove one into third place in the 1925 Grand Prix, then broke the Klausen mountain climb record, retired at San Sebastian, and duelled for the lead before breaking down in the 1926 Rome GP. The cars scored numerous subsequent successes on the Brooklands track, but their last appearance in a French GP was in 1931, when Jack Dunfee's car broke a drive shaft on the starting line. Another driven by W.T. McCalla won a road race in County Down, Northern Ireland, from the scratch mark as late as 1934, 10 years after that great French race the winner lost.

Specification
Engine
Six cylinders, in-line; bore and stroke, 67 × 94mm; capacity, 1988cc; twin overhead camshafts operating two valves per cylinder; unsupercharged, with single Solex carburetter, in 1923; Roots-supercharged, with Solex carburetter, in 1924–25. Bosch h-t magneto ignition; maximum power, 102bhp at 5000rpm unsupercharged; 138bhp at 5500rpm with supercharger.
Transmission
Three-speed gearbox and open propellor-shaft final drive in 1923; four-speed gearbox and torque-tube final drive, 1924–25.
Chassis
Pressed-steel side members; semi-elliptic springing front and rear; Hartford friction shock absorbers. Four-wheel brakes. Michelin tyres in 1923; Rapson tyres in 1924; Englebert tyres in 1925.
Dimensions
Wheelbase, 8ft 2in 1923, 8ft 6in 1924–25; front track, 4ft 1in 1923, 4ft 5in 1924–25; rear track, 4ft 1in 1923–25; dry weight, 1483lb in 1923, 1758lb in 1924–25.
Maximum speed
108mph in 1923, 125mph in 1924–25.

The 1924–25 Grand Prix Sunbeam, with Roots-supercharged 2-litre six-cylinder twin overhead camshaft engine which gave 138bhp at 5500rpm and brought it the Lyon lap record and a GP victory at San Sebastian, Spain. The brake servo on the four-speed gearbox and the torque tube final drive can be seen, also the wedge tail which had become fashionable in the 1920s

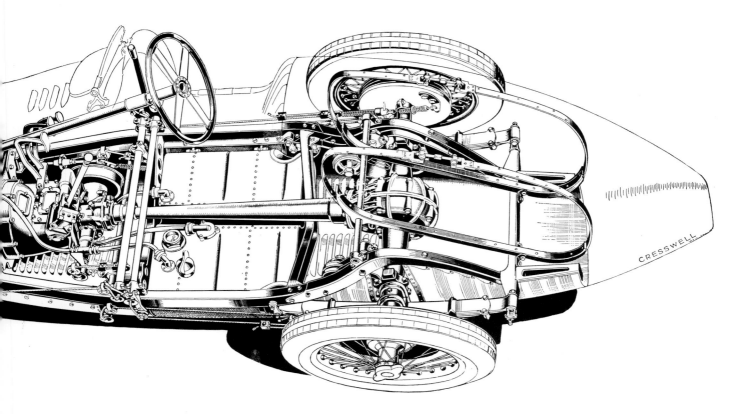

Alfa Romeo P2

'She was our beauty.'

Vittorio Jano

It may have soothed Louis Coatalen's conscience, should it have worried him, that Sunbeam was not the only marque to imitate the great works of Fiat. Another copyist, much closer to Turin, was Ing Giuseppe Merosi, chief designer for Alfa Romeo of Portello, Milan, who produced a Fiat-like twin-cam six-cylinder car called the P1 for 1923. Poor practice performance at Monza, a fatal accident and the ferocious pace of the winning Fiats decided Ing Nicola Romeo to scrap the cars. Then, sending 26-year-old Enzo Ferrari as intermediary, he lured the talented young Fiat engineer Vittorio Jano from Turin to design a new Grand Prix Alfa Romeo.

The resultant supercharged straight eight P2 emerged as a 'new broom' edition of the Fiat 805. Again there was a token difference in bore and stroke – 61 × 85mm (1987cc) for the P2 (the 805 engine measured 60 × 87·5mm) but the welded sheet-steel water jackets, twin overhead camshafts, 16 valves, roller bearing mains and big-ends and dry sump lubrication all remained. However, Jano chose spur gears aft of the engine to drive the camshafts rather than shafts and bevels, built up his engine in four blocks of two cylinders for easier casting and machining and specified a Roots supercharger geared at 1·23:1 instead of driving straight off the crankshaft.

The chassis followed the pleasing Fiat fashion of curving in at the rear, the body concealing the springs, while the front semi-elliptics still passed through eyes in the axle.

Jano avoided the rather tricky Fiat brake servo, preferring straight mechanical operation; for the rest, the wheelbase was the same (8ft 7·3in), front track fractionally wider, rear track identical and the weight about 44lb heavier. And the newer Alfa, distinguished by its bullnose radiator and the famous green *quadrifoglio* (four-leaf clover) on a white triangle, gave 134bhp to the Fiat's 130bhp, and was slightly faster at 139mph.

The first P2 made a surprise debut in the 200 Mile Cremona circuit race in the spring of 1924, when number one driver Antonio Ascari won at a highly impressive 98·3mph, set fastest lap at 100·8mph and clocked 121·16mph on the long 6·2-mile straight, thereby creating a new world 10km record. Four weeks later Campari led the Coppa Acerbo at Pescara until a tyre burst, and the P2's third outing was the all-important French Grand Prix at Lyon, where the 'new boys' from Portello met the seasoned Fiat, Sunbeam, Delage and Bugatti teams – and shattered the exalted Grand Prix world by their performance.

Despite Alfa's 'piracy' of Fiat technology and talent, it was noticeable that Nicola Romeo and Giovanni Agnelli were on amicable terms at Lyons. The Turin giant had supported racing since 1903, and with their vast production involvements possibly welcomed Alfa's intervention in support of Italy; Alfa Romeo, for their part, produced fewer, faster cars and were keen to enhance their image in racing. Right from the start the Alfas got to grips with the opposition, and

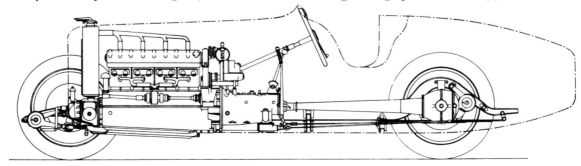

Classic arrangement: elevation of the 2-litre P2 Alfa Romeo, with semi-elliptically sprung chassis and front-mounted super-charged straight-eight twin-cam engine driving the rear wheels through a four-speed gearbox and torque tube

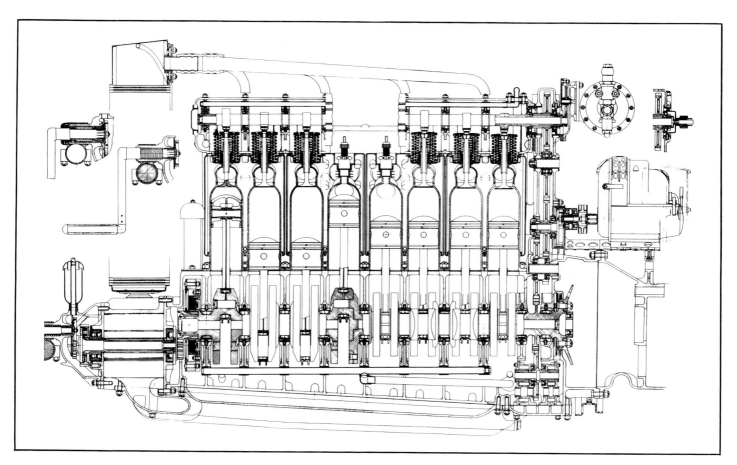

Above: *section of the P2 engine, showing its Roots-type supercharger, gear-driven off the front end of the roller-bearing crankshaft, and timing gears at the back of the unit, driving the twin overhead camshafts and Marelli magneto. This engine produced 134bhp at 5500rpm, later increased to 154bhp*

Left: *eleventh hour drama: after leading the 1924 Grand Prix at Lyon for over half its distance Antonio Ascari's P2 Alfa Romeo broke down only three laps from the chequered flag. Here his mechanic Giulio Ramponi tries desperately to restart it, but a cracked cylinder head was irremediable and Giuseppe Campari in another P2 came through to win for Alfa Romeo and Italy*

from half-distance were firmly in the lead, Ascari heading Campari, while the proud Fiats had dropped out with brake troubles. Then Ascari's P2 faltered and slowed only three laps from the flag, he and his mechanic Ramponi striving in vain to revive their car. Meanwhile team mate Campari passed to win the 503-mile classic, just a mile ahead of two Delages, with the third Alfa next home – a dramatic success for a new make.

A cylinder block had cracked on Ascari's car, but atonement came when he headed a triumphant one-two-three-four formation of P2s in the 497-mile Italian GP at Monza, while in the first 1925 classic, the European GP at Spa, Belgium, Ascari won again with Campari in train. He was all set for a third great victory in the French GP at Montlhéry when after a sudden rain shower his P2 slid an inch or so too close to the dangerous wood

37

Everybody happy: the Alfa Romeo pits after the 1924 Italian GP at Monza, where the P2s took the first four places. Left to right: mechanic Giulio Ramponi, master Alberto Ascari, his father Antonio who won the race, Nicola Romeo, chief of the Alfa Romeo concern, and another mechanic

Unassailable: Ascari and Campari in P2 Alfa Romeos roar away from the Delage opposition in the 1925 GP of Europe at Spa, Belgium. They took the first two places with ease

paling fence. A hubcap tangled, the car tore up 130 yards of fencing, then pitched over and Ascari was killed. Nicola Romeo ordered the withdrawal of the other cars, leaving the race to Delage.

The fourth and final Alfa Romeo victory as a factory team came in the 1925 Italian GP where the P2s finished one-two-five and were awarded the AIACR's first World Championship title. By then the engine had gained an extra 20bhp, largely through use of more potent fuel and a second Memini

carburetter, but the coming of the 1926–27 1½-litre Formula rendered the P2s redundant. Instead these splendid machines, superbly representative of the vintage Grand Prix era, ran in Formule Libre races and won 10 of them, with Achille Varzi's masterly victory with a modified P2 in the 1930 Targa Florio a triumphant finale before new Alfa Romeo designs superseded them.

Specification
Engine
Eight cylinders, in-line; bore and stroke, 61×85mm; capacity, 1987cc; twin overhead camshafts operating two valves per cylinder; Alfa Romeo Roots-type supercharger with single (later two) Memini carburetter; Marelli h-t magneto; maximum power, 134bhp at 5500rpm, rising to 154bhp at 5500rpm.
Transmission
Four-speed gearbox in unit with engine, torque-tube final drive.
Chassis
Pressed-steel side members; semi-elliptic springing front and rear; Hartford friction dampers. Four-wheel drum brakes. Pirelli tyres.
Dimensions
Wheelbase, 8ft 7·3in; front track, 4ft 3·25in, rear track, 4ft 1in; dry weight, 1646lb.
Maximum speed
139mph.

Type 35 Bugatti

'Were ever grace and purpose better combined?'

Charles Faroux

Until 1924 Grand Prix cars were very much the property of their makers, who paid for them, raced them, and reaped diverse benefits in marque prestige, increased sales of road models, and technological data. Then that great Italian-born, French-domiciled artist Ettore Bugatti changed the *status quo* by offering his racing cars for sale before they were even built. Such was his ingenuity and dedication, and so meritorious his cars, that the Type 35 Bugatti became the very mainstay of European motor racing between 1926 and 1931. The car attained no sensational peaks in power output or maximum speed, yet by getting the best from every bhp through superb handling and roadholding, it achieved a unique 'nimbleness' that brought innumerable victories.

At a Grand Prix bristling with novelties such as the P2 Alfa, the V12 Delages and the supercharged Sunbeams, the Type 35's debut at Lyon in 1924 was modest. Until then the Bugattis from Molsheim rated as clever but somewhat eccentric, as instanced by the 1922 'barrel-bodied' GP cars and the short-wheelbase 'tanks' of 1923. Visually the 1924 cars were a sensation, having exquisitely proportioned bodies, slender 'horseshoe' radiators, neat wedge tails *à la* Fiat, novel but attractive eight-spoked cast alloy wheels, and a striking 'heaven-blue' finish offset by polished metal parts.

Behind the aesthetics the straight eight 60 × 88mm 1955cc engine was a development of the Type 30 road model and the 1922–23 GP units. It had a single overhead camshaft operating three vertical valves in each cylinder, two of them inlets and one a large-diameter exhaust valve. The cylinders were of iron cast in two blocks of four with integral heads, and a finely executed built-up crankshaft ran in five large-diameter bearings, three in the centre of roller type, and the outer ones double-row ball races. The big ends also ran in roller bearings, with beautifully machined one-piece connecting

On aesthetics and effectiveness the Type 35 straight-eight Bugatti was a winner. Introduced in unsupercharged 95 bhp form at the historic 1924 French GP, this comely machine with its excellent road holding and fine handling was the first Grand Prix type car offered for sale to private owners and soon became the mainstay of European motor racing. At a time when performance demanded twin overhead camshafts and supercharging its unblown engine with single camshaft operating three valves per cylinder was retrogressive, but superchargers were fitted from 1926, when the cars were built in 1·5 litre, 2 litre and 2·3 litre forms, winning innumerable road races up to 1930

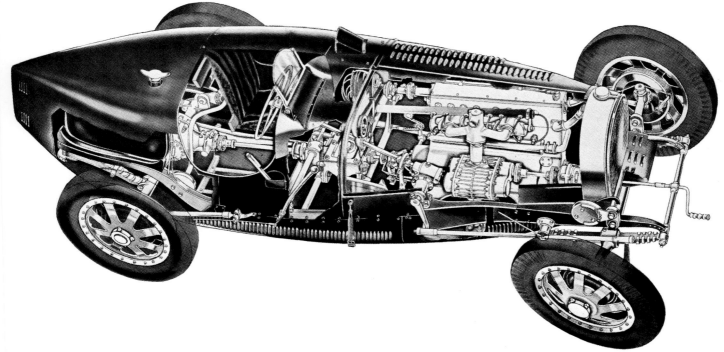

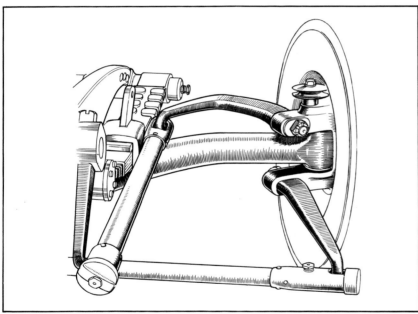

rods threaded on to the crankshaft during assembly.

Twin Zenith horizontal carburetters were employed, and a Scintilla magneto was driven off the rear end of the camshaft, protruding into the scuttle in typical Bugatti style. The edges of the head and block were severely squared, imparting the unique Bugatti sculptured effect, while also characteristic were the twin 'bunch of bananas' exhaust manifolds discharging into an under-chassis exhaust pipe. Engine output of the Lyon cars was about 95 bhp at 5000 rpm, which was modest when compared with their supercharged rivals though offset by a weight of only 1690 lb dry, good acceleration, cat-

like roadholding and ultra-precise steering.

Ettore Bugatti's design philosophy was a curious mixture of conservative and radical thought; he spurned twin overhead camshafts and hemi-heads, retained a separate gearbox, and considered supercharging 'unethical', thus giving his first 35s an in-built handicap. Yet his artistic finesse showed in numerous other ways, as in the elegant reversed quarter-elliptic rear springs and light alloy rear axle with radius arms, the deceptively delicate-looking front dumb irons, the tubular front axle (a masterpiece of skilful boring, forging and forming), the wet sump with aircooling by copper 'through' pipes, and the chassis side members of varying chord. And there were those alloy wheels with integral brake drums, reducing unsprung weight, improving heat dissipation and exposing the brake shoes for quick replacement during a long race. At Lyon a machining error and wrongly-vulcanised tyres (rushed from Dunlops by early airliner) brought an epidemic of thrown treads, and seventh and eighth places were thus Bugatti's best.

But ahead of them lay literally hundreds of wins to compensate. The first Type 35s reached private hands early in 1925, and the first amateur victory fell to Count Carlo Masetti in the Rome GP. A few weeks later works driver Costantini won the notorious Targa Florio, and Molsheim's golden age had begun.

The 1926–27 1½-litre Formula compelled *le Patron* to forget his prejudices against supercharging. He hired the Paris-based

Italian engineer Edmond Moglia to install a Roots-type blower on a new 60 × 66mm 1492cc Type 39, extracting approximately 110bhp at 5300rpm. This did not approach the power of the rival twin-overhead camshaft Delages and Talbots, but in 1926 Bugatti had the advantage on reliability and won the second World Championship title by taking three of the four qualifying races.

At the same time, conscious of Delage's Grand Prix threat and of the many free-formula events in the calendar, he also produced the 2261cc Type 35B, both blown and unblown, and then the 1990cc blown 35C. Between them this rich variety of *pur sang* automobiles made Bugatti the world's most successful racing marque. With amateur *Bugattisti* in dozens augmenting the factory team efforts, Type 35 wins came from all quarters and Molsheim were able to advertise that their cars had gained 577 *victoires* in 1926 and 806 a year later! Clearly such totals involved considerable barrel-scraping among minor events, but certain it is that between 1926 and 1931 (when a twin-cam GP Bugatti at last appeared) the ubiquitous Type 35 won 68 full-length races, including five Targa Florios, four French GPs, three GPs of Europe, three San Sebastian GPs, two Monaco GPs, one Italian and one German GP. And if in many cases there were few rivals, Bugatti preponderance was due to Bugatti excellence. At a time when art still had a say in racing car design, the Type 35 with its sublime workmanship was true artistry in metal, and justly rates today as the epitome of the classic vintage racing car.

Specification
Engine
Eight cylinders, in-line; bore and stroke, 60 × 88mm, capacity, 1991cc; single overhead camshaft operating three valves per cylinder; unsupercharged; twin Zenith carburetters; Bosch magneto; maximum power, approximately 95bhp at 5000rpm in 1924, rising to 130bhp at 5300rpm
Transmission
Separate four-speed gearbox and open propellor shaft.
Chassis
Steel side members; semi-elliptic front suspension; reversed quarter-elliptic rear suspension; friction dampers. Four-wheel drum brakes. Dunlop tyres in 1924; Michelin or Dunlop 1925 on.
Dimensions
Wheelbase, 7ft 10in; front and rear track, 3ft 11·25in; dry weight, 1690lb.
Maximum speed
110mph in 1924 form.
Model variants
Also produced as:
60 × 66mm, 1492cc Type 39, supercharged;
60 × 100mm, 2261cc Type 35B, supercharged;
60 × 88mm, 1990cc Type 35C, supercharged;
60 × 100mm, 2261cc Type 35T, unsupercharged.

'Bug' territory: two Type 35s in battle in the 1930 Monaco GP around the streets of Monte Carlo, Louis Chiron hard-pressed by W. Williams

41

1927 Grand Prix Delage

'Its designer was evidently imbued by the maxim "Nothing too much trouble, no expense spared." '

Laurence E. Pomeroy

European Champions: Robert Benoist at Brooklands winning the 1927 British GP, his fourth classic victory that season with the remarkable 1½-litre straight-eight Delage, looking unusual here with the exhaust silencer obligatory at the Weybridge track

While Ettore Bugatti was making his racing pay by selling Type 35s to customers, rival French manufacturer Louis Delage of Courbevoie took a different approach. A self-made man, when he had money he liked to spend it in flamboyant style. He lived the Paris social round to the full, and even bought himself a château on the Seine. He loved motor racing, and commissioned the building of complex, costly Grand Prix cars without demur. His 1923–25 2-litre V12s were fascinating machines, although they never got the better of Jano's fleet P2 Alfa Romeos, and were lucky to win two continental Grands Prix. They were reaching their peak only when the 1926 1½-litre Formula was announced, but Delage, undeterred by more expense, bade his design staff begin anew.

In charge was Ingenieur Albert Lory, who had assisted on the V12, the complexity of which probably persuaded him to opt for the more straightforward in-line eight. His design, works-coded the 15-S8, embodied one of the most remarkable engines of any time. His answer to friction was roller and ball bearings, totalling no less than 62. The one-piece, counterbalanced crankshaft ran in 10 split roller races, and the big ends, camshafts, an impressive train of 19 timing and drive gears, magneto and twin Roots superchargers were all pampered either with roller or ball bearings. The block and fixed head were a single iron casting with finely calculated porting – a considerable foundry achievement then – but apart from this the layout basically followed Fiat.

Dimensions were 55·8 × 76·0mm (1488cc), the twin overhead camshafts actuated two valves per cylinder at 100 degrees, and the unit could turn at a prodigious 8400rpm or more. For a 1½-litre the output was a remarkable 165bhp, running on a petrol/alcohol/benzol/ether mix with the blowers compressing at a mild 7·5psi. This magnificent, if rather weighty, unit drove the rear wheels through a multi-plate clutch and a five-speed gearbox in which fifth was an overdrive – a legacy from the older 2-litre V12. The chassis was underslung at the rear and ground

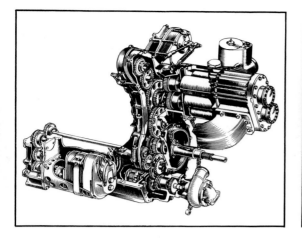

clearance was only four inches. Sparsely cross-braced, the frame was notably whippy, but Lory specified special high-tensile steel, deliberately allowing the chassis to 'undulate' over uneven surfaces and providing flexible mountings for the radiator, fuel tank, etc.

The 1926 GP rules helped to dictate the Delage's shape. A body width of at least 80cm (31·5in) containing two seats, but without the riding mechanic, was obligatory, and Lory offset this with as low a profile as possible. It is widely but falsely stated that the first 1½-litre Delage had an offset engine/drive line, whereas the very low seating position was achieved despite a central power train. In striving to keep width to the minimum, however, Lory rather cramped his drivers between the central propellor shaft and the exhaust pipe close to their right feet and arms – defects which were highlighted in the team's first race, the 1926 GP of Europe at San Sebastian, Spain, which took place in sweltering, equatorial heat. The hapless Delage pilots soon found their cockpits like ovens and their pedals almost

red hot from the nearby exhaust pipes. All pulled in, either to collapse or to bathe their cooked feet in cold water, while mechanics desperately cut air holes in the scuttles. Between stops the cars proved themselves fastest on the course and finally managed a truly valiant two-four-six placing.

For their second race, the first British GP at Brooklands, bowls of cold water were essential Delage pit equipment; one car retired with its bodywork burned through at the dash, but driver Wagner bravely shared another Delage with Sénéchal to win the race. The team gave the Italian GP a miss, and for 1927 Lory and chief assistant Gaultier wrought a remarkable metamorphosis. They turned the cylinder head round to transfer that incendiary exhaust system to the nearside, modified the supercharger layout, raised output to 170bhp and then, copying the 1926 straight eight Talbot, the whole power line was moved 100mm (just under 4in) to the left to give the drivers more room, while a new, inclined radiator was also fitted.

Third party in Delage's 1–2–3 victory in the 1927 French GP at Montlhéry, André Morel makes a pit stop

Albert Lory's legendary straight-eight Delage engine in which the crankshaft, connecting rods, camshafts, timing gears and many auxiliaries ran in roller or ball bearings, totalling 62 in all: 170bhp was realised at 8000rpm with remarkable reliability, running on a petrol/alcohol/benzol/ether fuel mixture with the Roots supercharger compressing at 7·5psi

After a preliminary canter at Montlhéry, where he won the GP de l'Ouverture, Delage's number one driver Robert Benoist scored four major victories in the French, Spanish, European and British GPs, the sleek blue cars proving utterly unassailable. The 1½-litre Formula then abruptly ended, so Louis Delage disbanded the team and sold his beloved cars to private owners. Malcolm Campbell scored easy wins in the 1928 Boulogne GP and 200 Miles Race at Brooklands, while between 1931 and 1933 Earl Howe won voiturette events at Dieppe, Avus and the Nürburgring. For 1936 one car was acquired by R.J.B.Seaman, who had it extensively rebuilt by Giulio Ramponi, former mechanic to the Alfa Romeo star Antonio Ascari. With new pistons, 12psi supercharger pressure, more potent fuel and other modifications, 185bhp was realised, while hydraulic brakes and lighter wheels and body were fitted, over 250lb being saved.

Allied with Seaman's skill, the 10-year-old car routed the more modern ERA and Maserati opposition in the 1½-litre class, winning the Douglas race in the Isle of Man, the Pescara and Swiss voiturette GPs and the 200 Miles Race at Donington. It was a fitting finale for a true masterpiece of 'expense-no-object' racing design.

Specification
Engine
Eight cylinders in-line; bore and stroke, 55·8 × 76mm; capacity, 1488cc; twin overhead camshafts operating two valves per cylinder; Roots-type supercharger with Cozette horizontal carburetter; Bosch h-t magneto; maximum power, 170bhp at 8000rpm.
Transmission
Five-speed gearbox in unit with engine; open propellor shaft.
Chassis
Pressed-steel side members; semi-elliptic springing front and rear; Hartford friction dampers. Four-wheel drum brakes, servo-assisted. Michelin tyres.
Dimensions
Wheelbase, 8ft 2·5in; track, 4ft 5in front and rear; dry weight, 1764lb.
Maximum speed
130mph.

1½-litre Miller '91'

'Miller could have made a lot more money if he hadn't cared so much about finish.'

Fred Offenhauser to Griff Borgeson

Before air travel made frequent transatlantic journeys feasible, American motor racing was naturally more 'isolationist' and differed greatly from that in Europe. The Indianapolis speedway set the fashion, producing numerous smaller counterparts in high-speed banked tracks, some metalled, others built of wood planking. They bred specialised cars in which gears, brakes and cornering agility were secondary to sheer, flat-out speed, the sole link with Europe being a lagging compliance with GP Formula capacity rules. Thus America maintained a 2-litre limit from 1923 to 1925, then switched to 1½-litres from 1926 to 1929, while ignoring weight and body restrictions and permitting single-seaters nine years before Europe did. The 1926 ruling produced one of America's most outstanding racing cars of all time, the Miller '91'.

The figures '91' simply denote 1½ litres in cubic inches, and both Millers and their arch-rivals Duesenberg built '91s'. Whereas the latter only ran team cars, however, the Miller company of Los Angeles, like Bugatti in Europe, built racing cars to sell. They were designed and built by the combined genius of Harry A. Miller, chief draughtsman Leo Goossen – the 'Ernest Henry' of the USA – and production engineer Fred Offenhauser. Like Ettore Bugatti, Miller was both artist and engineer, insisting on good proportions and fine finish as well as first-class engineering, being indifferent to cost so long as a car looked *right*. Aesthetically, Miller cars were jewels, but mechanically, too, they were exquisite.

The 91 engine was a compact twin overhead camshaft straight eight in two cast-iron blocks of four cylinders, with integral hemispherical heads and two valves per cylinder at 45 degrees. Dimensions were 55·5 × 76·2 mm (2·1 × 3 in) giving 1478cc (90·2cu in), and the crankcase was of slender barrel type in alloy, closely housing a counterbalanced five plain bearing crankshaft machined from

'Rooky' winner: 23-year-old Frank Lockhart, nominated a relief driver for the 1926 Indianapolis 500 a fortnight beforehand, confounded all critics by winning. The race was curtailed to 400 miles by rain, and Lockhart's 1½-litre eight-cylinder centrifugal-supercharged Miller '91' finishing almost three laps ahead of three more Millers

45

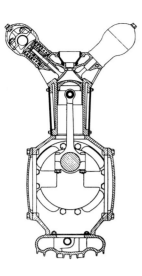

End section of the highly efficient twin overhead camshaft hemispherical-headed Miller '91' engine, which gave 154 bhp at 7200 rpm in its first 1926 form, an output sensationally raised in subsequent years to over 250 bhp

nickel molybdenum. Spur gears off the flywheel end drove a centrifugal-type supercharger at five times engine speed, i.e., at well over 30000 rpm. Centrifugal blowing was an American speciality developed as a result of track racing where power was required only at the top end of the engine speed range. The blower on the '91' compressed the mixture from a Miller or Winfield carburetter at a formidable 30 psi, and at 7200 rpm the 1926 engine delivered about 154 bhp, compared with the 165 bhp of that 'yardstick' of 1½-litre engines, the Delage.

Yet where the French car gained but 5 bhp in 1927 the Miller was progressively boosted to a works figure of 252 bhp, and, awe-inspiringly, to an estimated 285 bhp when master driver/tuner Frank Lockhart sensationally broke the world's flying mile record on Muroc dry lake, California, in 1927. Using his normal track single-seater with higher rear axle ratio, he averaged 164·009 mph and clocked a fantastic 171·02 mph in one direction – on just 1½ litres! The Miller would not have made a good Grand Prix racer, incidentally, for its torque band was too narrow and its three-speed gearbox and 'sprint' brakes inadequate for the rigours of a European road circuit, but on the high-speed American tracks it was supreme.

With the engine weighing only 230 lb, it scaled 1400 lb dry (Delage 1764 lb) and the lightweight, purposeful single-seat body was effectively set off by a shapely, plated 'bull-nose' radiator made by the Eskimo company. Alcohol and methanol fuels and higher compression ratios helped boost performance, as evidenced by Dave Lewis's 130·6 mph win in the 1927 Atlantic City 200 Miles race, where the irrepressible Lockhart made fastest lap at 147·7 mph. Remarkably, the 91 was built and sold both as a rear- or front-drive car. The latter application was naturally more complex, the engine being turned round to drive through the gearbox and frame-mounted differential, with two universal joints to each half-shaft, inboard brakes, and an inspired adaptation of the old 'de Dion' type axle in which the outer drive joints were linked with a built-up tubular cross beam, located by two pairs of forward-facing, quarter-elliptic leaf springs. Advantages of 'pull instead of push' on the speedway were very fast, constant-throttle cornering, lower build and less frontal area, and although Miller's front-drive 91 cost $15000 to the rear-drive's $10000, there were several buyers.

One front-drive exponent, Leon Duray,

won the 1927 Culver City 250 Miles at 124·7 mph, turned a qualifying lap at Indianapolis in 1928 at 124·01 mph (which stayed unbeaten until 1937), and set a new world closed circuit record at the Packard test track in Michigan at 148·17 mph. In 1929 Duray took two front-drive 91s to Europe, creating new 5- and 10-mile world records at Montlhéry at 139·2 and 135·33 mph respectively, then haplessly demonstrated the limitations of centrifugal supercharging in low-speed acceleration in the Monza GP where, despite leading the 1½-litre heat at one stage, he had to retire.

Race car sponsorship started in the 'States during the 1920s, ushering in the era of 'specials'. It was unfortunate, then, that when Miller sold a car they also sold its name. The impressive fact that Miller 91s won 25 major US races between 1926 and 1929, and countless lesser ones on the boards, ovals and dirt tracks, was thus largely lost on an American lay public who saw the victors only as 'Simplex Piston Ring', 'Boyle Valve', 'Packard Cable' and sundry other 'Specials'. But whatever the name on the scuttle, the heart of the immortal Miller 91 beat soundly underneath.

Specification

Engine
Eight cylinders, in-line; bore and stroke, 55·5 × 76·2 mm; capacity, 1478 cc; twin overhead camshaft operating two valves per cylinder; centrifugal supercharger; Miller or Winfield carburetter; Bosch h-t magneto; maximum power, 154 bhp at 7200 rpm, rising to over 250 bhp at over 8000 rpm.

Transmission
Three-speed gearbox in unit with engine; torque-tube final drive.

Chassis
Hand-beaten channel steel side members; semi-elliptic front and rear suspension; Hartford friction dampers. Four mechanical drum brakes. Firestone tyres.

Dimensions
Wheelbase, 8 ft 4 in; track, 4 ft 4 in front and rear; dry weight, 1415 lb.

Maximum speed
Approximately 140 mph in track racing trim.

Variants
Front wheel drive, with same engine turned about; twin quarter-elliptic front suspension with de Dion-type beam, Rzeppa universal joints.

Alfa Romeo 'Monoposto' P3

'Your car is fleet-footed, like a ballerina.'

Rudolf Caracciola to Vittorio Jano

Monoposto simply means 'single-seater' in Italian, but to countless admirers of historic racing cars it means the classic Alfa Romeo Tipo B, popularly, if unofficially, termed the P3, and designed by Vittorio Jano of P2 fame for the 1932 GP Formula. Since this limited races to five hours' duration, but left engine capacity unrestricted, one might expect Jano to have chosen a larger engine than 2·6 litres, especially when at least one formidable rival, the Maserati, had already gone up to 2·8 litres by 1931. But there were valid economic reasons for Jano's prescription of a 65 × 100mm straight eight. The world depression still hung heavily in 1932, money was tight everywhere, and Alfa Romeo had to watch their spending, even under the nationalistic spur of Mussolini's Fascist Government. The Type B was, in fact, a clever adaptation of old parts and new.

The previous year, Jano had produced the 65 × 88mm 2·3-litre straight-eight Monza model in sports and racing forms, and his new GP car embodied many features of that versatile design. The engine retained the cylinders cast in two alloy blocks, with steel liners and twin overhead camshafts. The stroke was extended to 100mm, giving 2654cc, and the central train of gears drove two Roots-type superchargers, one each side of the drive, a neat system used earlier by Emile Petit on his clever 1100cc straight-eight Salmson voiturette of 1927. A fixed head with valves at just over 100degrees echoed the 1926–27 Delage, but Jano avoided Lory's roller bearing extravaganza, the Type B's two-piece crankshaft running in 10 plain bearings. A Marelli magneto ousted the Monza's coil and distributor ignition, and light alloys figured wherever possible.

With the twin blowers compressing at 10psi, the power graph for this most handsome of engines showed 215bhp at 5600rpm. It went into a chassis retaining the 104in wheelbase and 55in front track of the Monza, but the side members, 5in at their deepest, were only 26in apart and the rear track was 'crabbed' at 53in. The single-seater body was the first in regular use in GP racing, although Brooklands and Indianapolis had seen one-place cars far earlier. The Monoposto's springing was by semi-elliptics all round, on delicate-looking outriggers at the rear, while the dry-plate clutch, four-speed gearbox and big mechanically operated brakes all derived from the Monza pattern.

Quite unique, however, was the final drive. In place of a central propellor shaft Jano employed his celebrated 'bifurcated' drive, in which two angled shafts in light steel torque tubes ran from a compact differential just behind the gearbox, driving

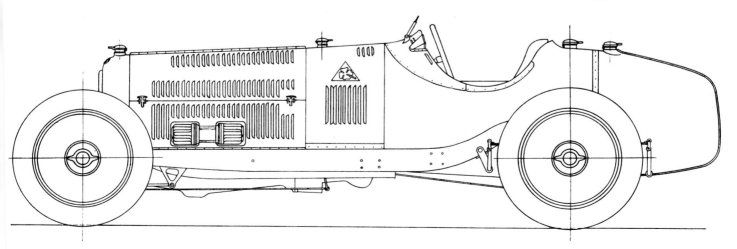

A novelty on the P3 was the
divided final drive by twin
propellor shafts from a
compact differential located
just behind the gearbox.
Objectives of the layout
included reduced unsprung
weight and easier access for
changing final drive ratios
without disturbing the
rear axle

Alfa Romeo developed the
1–2–3 habit early in the
new Monoposto's career.
Opposite, top: Varzi,
Chiron and Trossi line up
before the epic French GP
of 1934, when they routed
the new and still immature
German cars to place 1–2–3
in the order Chiron–Varzi–
Trossi. Opposite, below:
German team member
Caracciola stops for fuel and
tyres during the 1932
French GP at Reims where
they took the first three
places

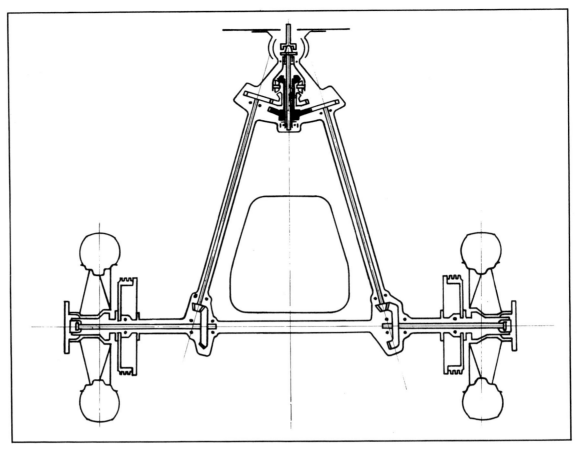

the rear axle by plain bevels and very short 'half' shafts. Primary gains were materially reduced unsprung weight, better power application to the rear wheels, and convenient access to the first-stage gears behind the differential for changing the overall drive ratio without stripping the rear axle. Light overall weight was a vital factor in the car's remarkably zestful performance on circuits all over Europe. It scaled 1545lb dry and approximately 1900lb laden; coupled with excellent low speed torque, this gave prodigious acceleration and a maximum of over 140mph.

Aesthetically, the car was about as fine a piece of Latin art as one could expect from Alfa Romeo and Vittorio Jano. If we regard his P2 as largely an improved Fiat, the P3 was surely his *capolavoro* – his masterpiece. In action there was nothing to touch it in 1932, and the Alfa Romeo drivers had no need for the telegrams *Il Duce* was wont to send them, ordering them to 'win for Italy'. Nuvolari did so in the Italian and French GPs and in the Ciano, Acerbo and Piedmont Cup races; Caracciola did likewise in the German and Monza GPs. Internal economic strictures kept Jano's lovely P3s dormant for the first half of 1933, but they were released to the Scuderia Ferrari by August in time for Fagioli to win at Pescara, Comminges and

Monza, and Chiron in Marseille, Czechoslovakia and Spain – score three-all.

1934 brought the new 750kg Formula, and the great confrontation with 'the German menace' from the all-independently sprung Mercedes-Benz and Auto Unions. The Alfas, their lissom lines plumped out to meet the new wider cockpit rules but supremely raceworthy with engines enlarged to 68 × 100mm (2905cc) won the dramatic opening round with a triumphant one-two-three in the French GP. Thereafter the cars from across the Rhine found reliability as well as devastating performance, and the Monoposto's golden days were done. When the Germans were absent the Alfas almost invariably won, scoring eight wins in 1934 including the Monaco and Tripoli GPs, while they also defeated Auto Union at Avus with a P3 wearing a specially streamlined body giving 12mph extra, devised by aeronautics expert Ing. Pallavicino of the Breda aircraft concern.

The cars were further updated for 1935, acquiring 71 × 100mm (3165cc) engines, Dubonnet independent front suspension, reversed quarter-elliptic rear springing and hydraulic brakes. The customary lesser wins fell their way, but they could not hold the Teutonic flood until that unforgettable July 28th when the incomparable Nuvolari ex-

ploited a damp and slippery Nürburgring and carried off the German GP itself from under the noses of five Mercedes and four Auto Unions – a glorious climax to the career of one of the greatest Grand Prix cars.

Specification
Engine
Eight cylinders, in-line; bore and stroke, 65 × 100mm; capacity, 2654cc; twin overhead camshafts operating two valves per cylinder; twin Roots-type superchargers, twin Memini carburetters; Marelli h-t magneto; maximum power, 215bhp at 5600rpm.
Transmission
Four-speed gearbox in unit with engine; 'bifurcated' drive by twin propellor shafts.
Chassis
Pressed-steel side members; semi-elliptic springing front and rear; friction dampers. Four-wheel drum brakes. Dunlop tyres in 1932, Englebert 1933-35.
Dimensions
Wheelbase, 8ft 8in; front track, 4ft 7in; rear track, 4ft 5in; dry weight, 1546lb.
Maximum speed
140mph.

Variants
Type B 2900, 1934: 68 × 100mm, 2905cc, 255bhp at 5400rpm; maximum speed, 162·5mph.
Type B 1935: 71 × 100mm, 3165cc, 265bhp at 5400rpm; three-speed gearbox; Dubonnet independent front suspension; reversed quarter-elliptic rear suspension; Ariston-Farina hydraulic brakes; maximum speed, 166mph.

Mercedes-Benz W25

'The Fuhrer has spoken. The 1934 GP Formula . . . must be a measuring stick for German knowledge and German ability.'

'Mannschaft und Meisterschaft'

Fifteen weeks after he had been appointed Chancellor of Germany, Adolf Hitler attended a motor race, the 1933 Avus Grand Prix on the fast motor road through the Grunewald outside Berlin. It was a bad race for Germany. Mercedes' works driver Otto Merz was killed in practice, while von Brauchitsch, the 1932 winner, could only manage sixth place owing to tyre trouble. The race fell to two deep-throated French 4·9-litre Bugattis which finished a sensational half-length apart, followed by three Italian Alfa Romeos. Hitler, unusually for a politician, was keen on motor racing and fully cognisant of its prestige value; the Avus result rankled, and shortly afterwards his government announced a special annual 450 000 marks (£41 500) subsidy for a German Grand Prix team, with extra bonuses for good race placings.

For Mercedes-Benz, already contemplat-ing a return to racing under the new 1934 Formula, the *Fuhrer*'s award clinched their decision. A bigger surprise was the news of a rival team, to be built by the new Auto Union group from Saxony to designs of Dr Ferdinand Porsche. There was thus domestic rivalry to add to the stimulus of national ambition, bringing to Europe the most exciting Grand Prix racing for decades, and sensational technological advances with it. The new Formula, with its *maximum* weight limit of 750 kg (1652 lb) minus fuel, oil, water and tyres, was a challenge to any enterprising manufacturer, and Mercedes got swiftly down to work.

Their new car, the W25A, broadly followed the *status quo* in the engine department, designers Hans Nibel and Max Wagner opting for a twin overhead camshaft straight eight of squarer dimensions (78 × 88 mm) and greater capacity (3360 cc) than the Monoposto Alfa

The new order: although teething troubles spoiled their first major outing in the 1934 French GP (Caracciola, seen here, retired after 16 laps) the new streamlined, all-independently sprung Mercedes-Benz W25s soon outmoded and outpaced (and outshrieked!) Alfa Romeo opposition in Grand Prix racing

Romeo which was its obvious first target. But it embodied Daimler-Benz' time-honoured construction with sheet-metal water jackets and valve ports welded on to separate, forged steel cylinders, combined in two groups of four. Each cylinder had four valves, and Mercedes upheld Fiat's all-roller bearing philosophy, using five split roller mains and one-piece roller big ends. A further apparent reversion lay in supercharging *through* the two twin-choke carburetters but, as pioneers in blowing, Mercedes had used this system since 1922 and a reliable 314 bhp at 5800 rpm on the first engines backed their conservatism.

The revolution was in the chassis. This had independent front suspension by wishbones and neat bell-cranks operating coil springs set horizontally within the front frame cross tube, a four-speed gearbox integral with the final drive, independent swing rear axles

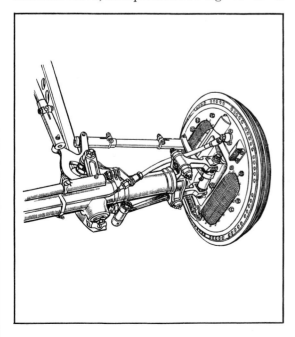

suspended on short transverse quarter-elliptic leaf springs, and Lockheed hydraulic brakes. None of these features on its own was entirely new, but collectively they were. With Auto Union also employing independent springing, Germany's 1934 cars emphatically ended the 40-year reign of 'cart spring' suspension. Vertical movement of Mercedes' first independent system was scarcely more than 2 in however, so that advantages were primarily in diminished wheelspin and greater acceleration, and certainly not in softer ride.

The chassis frame comprised two box-section side members pierced for lightness, cross-tied by tubes, and supporting the elegant all-alloy body on L- and T-framing copiously drilled to save weight. There was much drilling elsewhere, in brake levers and pedals, gear lever, seat supports, etc., indicating that Mercedes had difficulty in keeping within that 750 kg maximum weight barrier despite extensive use of costly light alloys. The whole car was superbly engineered and constructed by a large team of skilled specialists, transition from drawing board into metal taking them 10 months.

After extensive early tests in Italy and Germany, two cars ran their first race at the Nürburgring in the Eifelrennen in May 1934, driven by von Brauchitsch and the Italian Fagioli, with the famous Alfred Neubauer as team manager. Scraping through the weighing-in only by the desperate measure of removing all their elegant white paint, the Mercedes in bare aluminium confronted two Monoposto Alfa Romeos and two of the sensational rear-engined 16-cylinder Auto Unions. The result was a win for Brauchitsch, second for Auto Union, third for Alfa Romeo, and an early disciplinary problem for Neubauer when Fagioli abandoned his car in

Cost or complexity did not deter the Germans in their determination to win Grands Prix. Above, left: this offside view of the 1934–35 W25 shows the supercharger with its finned manifold, pierced box-section chassis and elaborate steering link above the friction-type shock dampers. Above: weight was a serious enemy in 1934, it being essential to drill components such as the gear lever and frame cross members to a gossamer degree to get the cars within the 750 kg (1652 lb) Formula limit

The W25 independent front suspension was by double wishbones and coil springs housed horizontally within the front cross tube of the chassis, worked by bell cranks

Mastery: Mercedes-Benz enjoyed a highly successful 1935 season, winning seven races with the improved 430 bhp W25B car. Here is the Italian member of the team, Luigi Fagioli, lapping a Maserati in the Monaco GP which opened the season; he won by over half a minute from two Alfa Romeo P3s

fine Latin dudgeon at being ordered to let his German team mate win on German soil.

After this encouraging dress rehearsal came the first major struggle in the French GP, with chastening defeat for the shatteringly fast and noisy, but still brittle, German cars by the seasoned Alfa Romeos. But the new double challenge could not long be stayed; Teutonic application, immense national enthusiasm and the *Fuhrer*'s spur had their way, and the rest of the 1934 season was a joint victory parade by Mercedes-Benz and Auto Union, the overall score being four-three in Unterturkheim's favour. Hitler decided to split his 450000 DM prize between the two teams; it scarcely covered early development costs, let alone operation of a full team all over Europe, but it was official encouragement. New fuel of methyl alcohol basis had bought useful extra bhp at Pescara in August, where Caracciola clocked 179·9 mph through a slightly downhill flying kilometre; for Monza a month later, Mercedes enlarged the W25 engine to 3·7 litres, then to 3·9 litres (82 × 94·5 mm) for the 1935 season. This was the W25B, whose drivers had some 430 bhp underfoot plus stronger transmission and ZF limited slip differentials, making good use of them all by winning nine of the 11 races they contested, including a satisfying one-two-four 'revenge' in the French GP they so humiliatingly lost the year before.

Specification

Engine
Eight cylinders, in-line; bore and stroke, 78 ×88 mm; capacity, 3360 cc; twin-overhead camshafts operating four valves per cylinder; Single Roots-type supercharger; Twin Mercedes carburetters; Bosch h-t magneto; maximum power, 314 bhp at 5800 rpm.

Transmission
Four-speed gearbox in unit with final drive.

Chassis
Box-section side members; independent front suspension by wishbones, bell cranks and horizontal coil springs; independent rear swing axles with quarter-elliptic springs; friction dampers. Lockheed hydraulic four-wheel drum brakes. Continental tyres.

Dimensions
Wheelbase, 8 ft 11 in; front track, 4 ft 10 in, rear track, 4 ft 7 in; dry weight, 1626 lb.

Maximum speed
175 mph.

Variants
Engine enlarged to 82 ×88 mm, 3710 cc, 348 bhp, late in 1934.
Engine enlarged to 82 ×94·5 mm, 3990 cc, 430 bhp, for 1935 (W25B).

Auto Union D-type

'One has to be rather more careful with a rear-engined car, to concentrate even more, and take fewer liberties.'

Nuvolari through an interpreter to John Dugdale, 'The Autocar'

The mid-engined Grand Prix car seems so logical now that it is hard to realise that, despite a six-year exposure to the layout in the 1930s, the racing world ignored its potential and remained happily front-engined for another 20 years. As practised by Auto Union of Germany in 1934–39, however, the principle achieved no clear-cut superiority warranting a design revolution, although ironically it was the compatriot front-engined Mercedes-Benz which dimmed the Auto Union message by largely eclipsing its performance, while outside critics deprecated its virtues and over-emphasised its vices.

The Austrian Dr Ferdinand Porsche had persuaded Auto Union AG of Zwickau, a combine of four Saxon marques, DKW, Wanderer, Audi and Horch, to adopt rear-engined location in a GP car. They were not complete pioneers – a gallant Benz three-car attempt in the 1923 Italian GP wilted before the scorching Fiat pace and finally withered through financial strictures – but Auto Union raced hard through two GP Formulae with the major car organs where they are today, with engine behind the driver and gearbox behind the final drive. But for suspension and handling limitations, inevitable at that time of early probing into a new science, designers might well have turned much sooner to the mid-engined layout.

The 3-litre D-type Auto Union of 1938 represents the second phase of the firm's thinking. The 1934–37 750kg cars embodied Dr Porsche's design philosophy of a big, lazy, lightly stressed engine, his 45 degree V16, which grew from 4·4 to 6 litres and gained them 18 Formula race wins in four seasons to Mercedes' 22. The new 1938–40 Formula posed new problems with a top capacity limit of 3 litres for supercharged cars, obliging Auto Union to seek performance by efficiency rather than cubic capacity. The new rules of the AIACR (predecessor of the FIA) intended cars from 666cc to 4500cc,

420 horsepower plus the genius of Tazio Nuvolari gained Auto Union two outstanding 1938 victories over Mercedes-Benz in the Italian and Donington GPs. Here is the Italian 'Maestro' at work in Britain's Grand Prix event with the 3-litre V12 D-type

53

blown or unblown, to have an equal chance under a sliding weight scale, but both Auto Union and Mercedes-Benz plumped unhesitatingly for supercharging regardless of complexity and heavier fuel consumption, and both chose 60 degrees V12 engines. This apart, the two cars differed widely.

Never so strong in technical or financial resources as their Unterturkheim rivals, Auto Union encountered dire new problems at a crucial time. Dr Porsche had left them to devote his time to Germany's new Volkswagen project and then, early in 1938, they lost their star driver Bernd Rosemeyer in a foolish record foray. Porsche was replaced by Prof. Eberan von Eberhorst, but no-one could replace the brilliant Rosemeyer, whose death completely 'threw' the team. Auto

Union seriously considered withdrawing from racing, but finally their director of engineering, Dipl. Ing. Werner, persuaded them to resume 1938 racing plans.

Where the 16-cylinder engine had one central camshaft and pushrods, the new V12 employed a novel three-camshaft layout with one central camshaft operating all 12 inlet valves, and one camshaft per head operating the exhaust valves. A Hirth built-up crankshaft ran in eight ball-bearing mains, cylinder dimensions were 65 × 75mm, a big vertical Roots-type supercharger sucked through twin Solex carburetters, and initial output was 420 bhp at 7000 rpm. A five-speed gearbox with ZF limited slip differential was behind the rear axle line, the drive shaft from the engine passing below. The

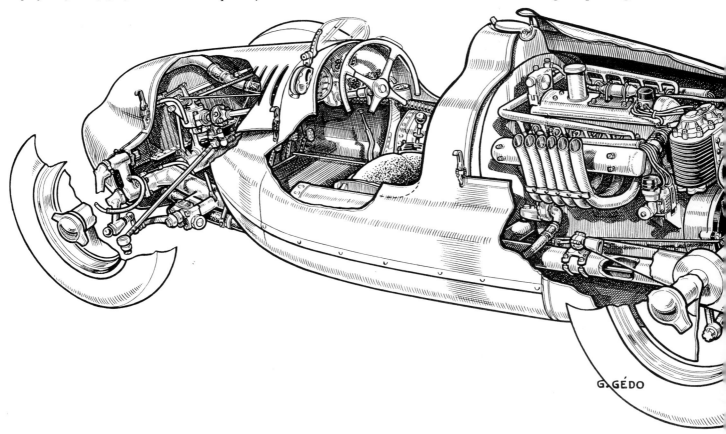

G. GÉDO

chassis followed Porsche pattern in being of 'ladder' type, its wheelbase 6in shorter at just over 9ft. The Doktor's favourite independent front suspension by trailing links and torsion bars also remained, but his rear swing axles gave way to a de Dion type. This was adapted from Dr Siebler's 1936 Horch road-car design, but used longitudinal torsion bars housed in the frame tubes plus a lateral Panhard rod and radius arms.

As before, the radiator was in the nose, but von Eberhorst replaced the V16's deep fuel tank between driver and engine with side tanks, and with the space thus gained and the shorter V12 engine, moved the driver's seat further back to an almost central position. Collectively these measures improved weight distribution, road holding and driver control, changing a precipitate oversteerer to a fundamental understeerer. Overall weight proved fractionally over the 1870lb minimum dictated by the Formula, and compared comfortingly with Mercedes' 1995lb. The first bodywork was a dismal adaptation of the old 1937 type with the new side tanks, and owing to Auto Union's early troubles the new cars missed the first three 1938 races, then made a disastrous debut in the French GP when both cars retired on the first lap.

Zwickau morale was rock bottom when Direktor Werner persuaded the world's greatest driver, Tazio Nuvolari, to join the team in time for the German GP. An infinitely better looking body offering materially less drag was also produced and a new spirit galvanised the Saxon team. It took the *Maestro* three races to get into 'the rear-engined groove', and then he rounded on Mercedes to win the Italian GP at Monza, and beat them again in the Donington GP – the British GP in all but name.

For 1939 the D-types gained two-stage supercharging and 485bhp at 7000rpm, but as Mercedes had also 'gone two-stage' some epic duels resulted. Nuvolari broke his own car while breaking Mercedes' pacemaker in the French GP, leaving another Auto Union to win, Stuck won a 'demonstration' GP of Bucharest, and Nuvolari had the last word by beating Mercedes in the Jugoslav GP at Belgrade on the very day France and Britain declared war on Germany.

Four wins in a season and a half was no epic, but with Nuvolari a matchless number one driver and von Eberhorst eroding the myth of rear-engined 'uncontrollability' race by race, who knows what path future designers might have taken? Alas, the man who started it all, Adolf Hitler, also stopped it by bringing war instead, and the rear-engined Auto Unions never raced again.

Specification
Engine
60 degree V12; bore and stroke, 65 × 75mm; capacity, 2990cc; triple camshafts operating two valves per cylinder; single vertical Roots supercharger; twin Solex carburetters; twin Bosch magnetos; maximum power, 420bhp at 7000rpm, rising to 485bhp with two-stage supercharging in 1939.
Transmission
Five-speed gearbox in unit with final drive; ZF limited slip differential.
Chassis
Tubular side members; independent front suspension by trailing links and transverse torsion bars in frame cross tube; de Dion-type rear suspension with longitudinal torsion bars in frame side members and radius arms; Fichtel & Sachs hydraulic front dampers, friction rear dampers. Lockheed hydraulic four-leading shoe brakes. Continental tyres.
Dimensions
Wheelbase, 9ft 0·1in; front and rear track, 4ft 7·1in; dry weight, 1875lb.
Maximum speed
192mph.

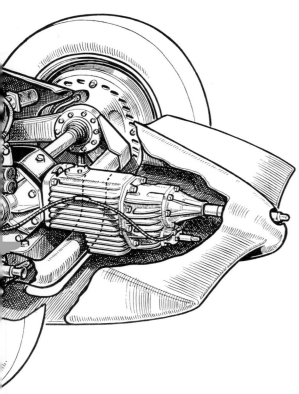

Maserati Type 8CTF

'It looked like it would run for ever—and fast.'

Wilbur Shaw

Opposite, top: end section of the 69 × 100mm twin-cam 8CTF Maserati engine, which produced a reliable 350bhp at 6000 rpm

Opposite, bottom: the 8CTF's independent front suspension by C-section wishbones and longitudinal torsion bars was totally new to Indianapolis racing

Ingenuity, love for 'having a go' at long odds, optimism and parsimony all contributed to the creation of the 8CTF Maserati, a car built for Grand Prix racing but which started an Indianapolis revolution. When the new 3-litre supercharged/4½-litre unsupercharged GP Formula was announced for 1938–40, most non-Germans were resigned to a continuation of Mercedes-Auto Union domination. The French hopefully planned some unblown 4½-litre cars, while Alfa Romeo, disillusioned, practically gave up trying.

As for the illustrious but taciturn *Fratelli* Maserati of Pontevecchio, Bologna, they had retreated to the 1½-litre voiturette class and were doing very nicely without incurring the heavy expense necessary to combat the highly scientific German bolides. In 1937, while Maserati's small, six-cylinder *monoposti* were selling briskly to private owners, they quietly developed a faster, four-cylinder works model, the 4CM, with which their number one driver, Count Trossi, scored several useful successes. Its twin overhead camshaft engine had the classic bore and stroke of 69 × 100mm, as on the now outdated 2·9-litre eight-cylinder GP Maseratis of 1933–34, which doubtless helped keep spares

costs down when the little 175bhp four broke, as Maseratis were inclined to do under stress.

Then something of great importance happened to the small but dedicated Bologna marque. Big industrialist Adolfo Orsi made a take-over bid for the works (he was really after their sparking plug business), and the brothers Ettore, Bindo and Ernesto accepted, it being agreed that they would continue building Maserati racing cars, but in Modena rather than Pontevecchio. By exchanging their valued independence for security, the *fratelli* gained an extra plum – a special, limited budget to build two new 3-litre Grand Prix cars and challenge the *Tedeschi* in 1938 – which they greatly yearned to do.

With time and cost both limited, they could not afford complex 12-cylinder engines or sophisticated chassis and suspensions. Conditioned by years of 'making do' with what they had, however, they happily resorted once again to expediency to produce their GP car. The resultant Tipo 8CTF had virtually a 10 per cent enlargement of their 1937 4CM voiturette chassis, with similar box-section welded chassis, torsion bar independent front suspension, and quarter-elliptically sprung rigid rear axle. Its straight-

Showing them how: a stagnant American racing car industry was severely jolted in 1939, when Mike Boyle imported this 3-litre straight-eight Maserati 8CTF for Wilbur Shaw to drive in the Indianapolis 500. Shaw won by almost 2 minutes in 1939, and won again in 1940 by almost a lap. In 1941 he had a lap lead with 120 miles to go when a tyre burst and a wheel collapsed, spoiling his 'hat trick'

56

eight engine consisted of two 4CM cylinder blocks with a one-piece cylinder head, mounted in line on a new bottom end carrying a five plain-bearing crankshaft. The voiturette's single Roots-type blower and Memini twin-choke carburetter were duplicated, and even the power output was exactly double – 350 against 175bhp at 6000rpm, promising about 170mph.

A novel chassis feature was a cast aluminium oil tank which also served as a support for fuel tank and seat, and as chassis cross bracing; braking was hydraulic all round, dry weight was 1898lb (the rival Mercedes scaled over 2000lb), and this Maserati with its shapely nose and tail and paired exhaust pipes looked a very handsome rival to Germany's 'silver arrows' though costing considerably less. Two cars were ready in time for the 1938 Tripoli GP on the ferociously fast Mellaha circuit in North Africa. Drivers were Achille Varzi and Count Trossi, and although Varzi's car failed early, Trossi spurted sensationally past the Mercedes trio to lead the race on lap eight – a gallant gesture, although the 8CTF quickly wilted and died after its round of glory.

Most unfortunately, Orsi's budget did not permit a full season of racing so that the car never developed the necessary stamina. It appeared in three Italian races that year, invariably performing brilliantly but briefly. At Leghorn, Trossi led the Mercedes again, and again blew up; at Pescara, Luigi Villoresi took over from a weary Trossi, worked up to second place, made fastest lap, then blew up. At Monza, Trossi nursed the 8CTF home to its first finish, in fifth place. For their final 1938 effort Maserati rushed a car to the Donington GP in Britain; the gearing was wrong, Villoresi drove too hard, and broke a piston.

But the 8CTF's days of glory were to come in an unexpected sphere. Rules for the Indianapolis 500 Miles race were changed in 1938 to conform with the European GP Formula in a fruitless effort to bring racing in the two continents closer together. The American Mike Boyle ordered 'the latest Maserati' for Wilbur Shaw to drive at Indianapolis, but the *Fratelli* sold him a 1½-litre (91cu in) Type 6C voiturette! Shaw declined to race it, so Boyle tried again for 1939, sending his master mechanic Cotton Henning to Italy to get 'a real 183-inch car'. This time it *was* an 8CTF, with a 365bhp engine and single large-diameter exhaust pipe in place of the dual GP system.

Boyle vetted the car meticulously, fitted

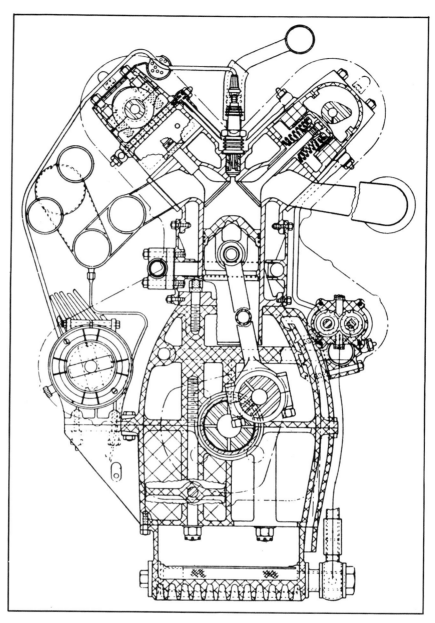

For a European GP car, the Maserati 8CTF found itself in some unusual situations. Here is the car originally sent over in 1940 for two Frenchmen to drive at Indianapolis, breaking the 1946 Pike's Peak 12·5 mile mountain record driven by Louis Unser

its duralumin wire wheels with Firestone tyres, and to ensure reliability reduced the blower pressure and hence the power, getting 350bhp on methanol. Making full use of the Maserati's four-speed gearbox, Shaw rocketed ahead at the start and finally outpaced the fierce American single-seaters to win the 500 by two minutes. It was the first European car victory since Peugeot's in 1919, but Wilbur Shaw proved it was no flash in the pan by winning again in 1940. A hat trick in 1941 was foiled when an unbalanced wheel broke up at three-quarters distance when he held a lap's lead, but the sleek Boyle Maserati left an indelible mark on Indianapolis. The value of independent front suspension, a good chassis and clean, low-drag bodywork really got home, and 'the Maserati shape' became familiar wear in early post-war '500's.

Back home in Europe, the works 8CTF gave the Germans one more fright before war ended motor racing. It was in the 1939 German GP, run in treacherous 'wet and dry' conditions at the Nürburgring. Paul Pietsch in the Maserati ran third on lap one, then took the lead on lap two – a splendid situation which lasted only one round, when plug and front brake troubles cost him over six minutes in four pit stops. He finally got back to third place, the 8CTF's best GP showing. During Italy's 'twilight peace' before 1940, Maseratis built another 3-litre in the same chassis, the 8CL, using two 1939 16-valve 78×78mm voiturette blocks and getting 415bhp at 6400rpm. It promised well on paper but accomplished little, the first car being crashed at Indianapolis in 1940, while a second 8CL built in 1946

placed seventh at Indianapolis in Villoresi's hands, won a minor 157-mile race at Lille the same year, and another at Mar del Plata, Argentina, in 1947. Formula changes in 1948 made it redundant, but in any case the 8CL never enjoyed the cachet of two straight Indianapolis victories as did its elder long-stroke brother, the 8CTF.

Specification
Engine
Eight cylinders, in-line; bore and stroke, 69×100mm; capacity, 2992cc; twin overhead camshafts operating two valves per cylinder; twin Roots-type superchargers; two Memini twin-choke carburetters; Scintilla Vertex magneto; maximum power, 350bhp at 6000rpm in 1938, 365bhp at 6400rpm in 1939.
Transmission
Four-speed gearbox in unit with engine; torque tube final drive.
Chassis
Welded box-section, underslung at rear. Independent front suspension by wishbones and longitudinal torsion bars; non-independent rear suspension by quarter-elliptic springs and radius arms to live rear axle. Friction front shock absorbers, hydraulic at rear. Lockheed hydraulic four-wheel brakes. Pirelli tyres in Europe; Firestone at Indianapolis.
Dimensions
Wheelbase, 8ft 11·2in; front track, 4ft 4·8in; rear track, 4ft 5·5in; dry weight, 1898lb (GP cars), 1937lb (Indianapolis).

1939 Mercedes-Benz W154

'When all 33 cars were warming up . . . there was one that could be heard above them all . . . the 12 cylinder German-built Mercedes.'

'Indianapolis Star' report of 1948 500 Miles race

Of all the exciting cars produced during the exciting 1934–39 Grand Prix period, the 3-litre V12 Mercedes-Benz W154 must rank as the ultimate in purpose building. Never did a car look so ruthlessly right, nor emit such stirring blown multi-cylinder noises. Never, indeed, could a car have achieved Germany's aim of impressing Europe with her technological prowess more effectively than this awe-inspiring piece of propaganda machinery. Yet the political motives behind such an instrument should not sour admiration for its design, execution and performance, not its superb beauty hide the inescapable limitations of nearly 40 years ago.

When the 3-litre-blown/4½-litre-unblown Formula of 1938–40 was announced, Mercedes-Benz laid down an all-new 60 degree four-cam V12 engine rather than further develop their basically 1934 straight-eight

design which had served so well under the 750kg rulings. Unlike Auto Union, they believed they could compensate for the extra weight and complication of a front-mounted engine by sheer power, better suspension and easier handling. In the then-current state of the art they were largely proved right. In 1938 form, designated the M154, the 67 × 70mm 2962cc 48-valve engine had the usual Mercedes welded cylinder construction, mercury-cooled exhaust valves, one-piece seven-roller bearing crankshaft, and two duplicated Roots-type superchargers compressing mixture *from* a Mercedes carburetter rather than plain air *into* one as had so long been their custom. Initial output was 425bhp at 8000rpm, progressively rising with development during the 1938 season to approximately 466bhp.

As installed into the W154 car, the engine

The 3-litre Mercedes-Benz in its 1939 two-stage supercharged form was impressively packed with machinery. The four-cam 12-cylinder engine, producing a strident 484bhp at 7500rpm, was installed desaxé at the front of the tubular chassis, the drive shaft being angled to pass alongside the driver's seat. A five-speed transverse gearbox was in unit with the final drive, and de Dion-type rear suspension was employed

R E POULTON

First of five Grand Prix wins for the 1939 car in that war-shortened season fell to Hermann Lang at Pau, France

was mounted *desaxé* in the welded tubular chassis, i.e. with transmission line angled near-diagonally (as on the 1926–27 GP Talbot) to gain more room for the driver's seat alongside the propellor shaft, which drove to a five-speed transaxle-cum-final drive. The suspension derived from the highly successful 5·6-litre 1937 car which broke a 50-year tradition that racing car road springs had to be hard; it was independent at the front by wishbones and coil springs, and of de Dion type at the rear, with longitudinal torsion bars and C-section radius arms. There was now some 3–3·5in vertical movement in the springing compared with the 2in of the old W25, with vital gains in roadholding, stability and ride.

The new V12 had a voracious thirst at something like 2mpg for a potent fuel comprising 86 per cent methyl alcohol, plus nitro-benzole, acetone and sulphuric ether. This was carried in two tanks, one in the tail, the other in the scuttle, and, as the fuel emptied, the changing weight distribution was offset by lever adjustment of the rear damper ride settings by the driver. The formidable total of 105 gallons carried helps to explain a starting weight of over 2688lb, but despite this the W154 was devastatingly fast

and won six races in five countries during 1938.

Two defeats by the rear-engined Auto Unions at the close of the season added urgency to Unterturkheim's customary winter improvement programme, when engineers Wagner, Heess and Uhlenhaut extracted an extra 18bhp and more torque by adopting two-stage supercharging and modifying the valve timing. Oil scavenging problems were alleviated by increasing the number of pumps to no fewer than nine, weight was cut down by about 150lb, and ingenious new turbo-cooled brakes were fitted. The radiator, actually containing ethylene glycol as the coolant rather than water, was placed further forward, with an extra cooler for the fuel, and all the machinery was enclosed in a new low-drag, 'sharknosed' body of sinister beauty.

This new silver projectile, a kind of 'Mark 2' W154, carried off the Pau, Eifel, Belgian, German and Swiss Grands Prix in the shortened 1939 season. Engine fragility cost Mercedes one Grand Prix, and driver temperament another, but in general these mechanical omnivores epitomised the totally professional, scientific approach to success for which Daimler-Benz were so famous. Al-

though it did not quite equal the all-out 200mph maximum of the 1937 5·6 litre car, it was overall the fastest circuit car produced in the six-year 'Teutonic age' of Grand Prix racing.

For over a decade after its peak, the W154 was regarded as the *ne plus ultra* of racing cars, but a chastening demonstration of its limitations came on the single occasion that Unterturkheim tried racing the car after the war, in two Argentine races for the President Peron and Eva Peron Cups at Buenos Aires in 1951. Despite a three-car team including the great Fangio and 1939 Champion Hermann Lang they were twice defeated by Gonzalez driving a private 2-litre supercharged V12 Ferrari. On a tight, twisty little course the German cars were, in truth, oversized, overweight and overpowered, and with fuel and carburation troubles to embarrass them further, the mighty 'silver arrows' of yesteryear were humbled by the nimble little Ferrari. Another V12 brought out of Europe and sold to a private owner in the USA ran twice in the Indianapolis 500 Miles Race in 1947 and 1948, but failed each time, primarily through lack of proper works attention and comprehension of a very complex design.

Specification
Engine
60 degree V12; bore and stroke, 67 × 70mm; capacity, 2962cc; Four overhead camshafts operating four valves per cylinder; mercury-filled exhaust valves; single-stage supercharging in 1938, two-stage in 1939; twin Bosch magnetos; maximum power, 425 bhp at 8000rpm in 1938, rising to 484bhp at 7500rpm in 1939.
Transmission
Five-speed transverse gearbox in unit with final drive; ZF limited-slip differential.
Chassis
Tubular side members; independent front suspension by wishbones and coil springs; de Dion rear axle with torsion bar suspension; hydraulic dampers. Hydraulic brakes with turbo-extractor drums in 1939. Continental tyres.
Dimensions
Wheelbase, 8ft 11·25in; front track, 4ft 10in; rear track, 4ft 7in; dry weight, 1995lb.
Maximum speed
192mph.

A close-up of Caracciola's car at Reims during practice for the 1939 French GP emphasises the tightness of the cockpit and the need for a detachable steering wheel, seen hanging on the right-side mirror

Alfa Romeo Type 158/159

'The latest car is a beauty. A car of real class.'

Emilio Villoresi, 1939

'What a gem she was.'

Juan-Manuel Fangio, 1950

As Germany's Grand Prix challenge grew rapidly to total domination, other marques with lesser resources began a strategic withdrawal. Bugatti exploited sports car racing, Maserati switched to 1½-litre voiturettes, and even Alfa Romeo, proud leaders until 1934, took up this 'Junior' class at the instigation of Enzo Ferrari, who managed their racing from Modena. Despairing of ever breaking the German hold on Formula racing, he put Jano's former chief *aide*, Gioacchino Colombo, to the task of designing a new 1½-litre straight-eight *vetturetta*, and soon Alfa Romeo took official interest. On May 7th, 1938 the prototype, skimpy and unpainted, was tried out at Monza by test driver Enrico Nardi, and less than three months later four cars lined up for the Coppa Ciano Junior race at Leghorn. Beautiful little machines in Italian red, the *Alfettas*, as they were dubbed, delighted the crowd by scoring a one-two victory, and although teething troubles dogged them at

Pescara and Modena, they scored another one-two at Monza, bringing new heart to Italian motor racing.

Designated simply the Tipo 158 (*1·5 litri, 8 cilindri*), Colombo's new creation was a clean, attractive design having a 58 × 70mm, 1479cc in-line eight-cylinder 16-valve engine, twin overhead camshafts, a single Roots blower, and an output at Leghorn of 195 bhp at 7000 rpm. The exhaust valves had sodium-cooled stems, and a light but sturdy crankshaft ran in eight plain bearings. As on their 1935–37 Tipo C GP cars, the four-speed gearbox was integral with the final drive, the propellor shaft lowered by double reduction gears. The frame was tubular, usefully braced by the engine and final drive unit, and suspension was independent all round by transverse leaf springs, through Porsche-type trailing links at the front end and swing axles at the rear.

In their first race of 1939, the 158s met un-

A cutaway of the first Alfa Romeo Type 158, produced in 1938 as a 1½-litre racing voiturette, with an initial output of 180–190 bhp

Two of the illustrious 'three Fs' making up the 1950 Alfa Romeo team – Farina leading Fagioli in the European GP at Silverstone. Fangio was ahead of his colleagues at this stage, but later retired with engine trouble

Swiss Prix de Berne. Yet the Tripoli defeat rankled, and when the 1940 race came round, the Germans being absorbed in more deadly contests, Alfa Romeo took a rather empty 'revenge' with a one-two-three win at 128·14mph, over 5mph faster than the 'Mini-Mercs' in 1939. Then the war finally involved Italy and the *Alfettas* were walled up in a cheese factory at Melzo, near Milan, for the duration.

When racing resumed in 1946, the Tipo 158 found itself elevated to Grand Prix rank through Formula changes and the disappearance of the German teams. Failure of both Alfas first time out at St Cloud caused a flutter, but Portello soon established the supremacy of their famous *quadrifoglio*. Dr Orazio Satta converted the engines to two-stage supercharging, which increased power to 245bhp and ensured sweeping victories at Geneva, Milan and Turin. 1947 brought 275bhp and four more wins at Berne, Spa, Bari and Milan, and total Alfa domination continued in 1948 with four further firsts at Berne, Reims, Turin and Monza. By then the power curve read 310bhp at 8500rpm, with the Alfa engineers assuring an anxious board that there was 'plenty left'.

In 1949 Portello took a year off racing, sated with victory, busy on a new road model, and shattered by the deaths of their three top-line drivers, Varzi and Wimille in crashes, Trossi through illness. When the raucous blood-red cars reappeared they met new opposition from the young marque Ferrari, yet 1950 proved to be the 158's 'golden year'. They now had 350bhp at 8600rpm on call from that remarkable engine, and with in-

Driver's view of the 159, final version of Alfa's remarkable 1500, showing the trailing link front suspension and economy of instruments.

expected opposition in the Tripoli GP which, like other Italian events that year, had switched from 3- to 1½-litre rulings. Mercedes-Benz decided that this prestigious and highly endowed race warranted the considerable expense and effort of building special new 1½-litre V8s of almost 250bhp. Colombo had given the 158 engines needle roller main bearings by then, improved the lubrication and raised output to 225bhp at 7500rpm, but at Tripoli they suffered dire overheating and could not prevent a sensational one-two Mercedes triumph at 122·9mph, only one *Alfetta* surviving, a tardy third.

Alfa Romeo quickly cured the overheating, found reliability and still more power, and fitted purposeful new bodies with broader noses and head fairings. They took two home wins (one-three at Leghorn, one-two-three-four at Pescara), then scored brilliantly in the

63

Fangio in Alfa Romeo No. 4 leading the 1951 French GP at Reims. When ignition trouble assailed his car, the Argentinian took over Fagioli's Alfa to win from two 4½-litre Ferraris

solent ease won all 11 races they contested, including the classic British, Monaco, Swiss, Belgian, French and Italian GPs. For his part in these their number one driver, 'Nino' Farina, emerged the first World Champion.

But the Ferrari menace deepened in 1951 with full 4½-litre unsupercharged machines, and the *quadrifoglio* stable prepared for battle,

mustering a staggering 420bhp at 9600rpm, installing extra fuel tanks and changing the swing rear axles for a de Dion layout. Called the 159 in this form, these astonishing 1500's now gulped their potent Shell alcohol diet as greedily as the 1939 German 3-litre cars at under 2mpg, and with a laden weight now up to 2380lb 'middle-age spread' and 'breathlessness' began to show. They won the first three championship rounds at Berne, Spa and Reims, but then came their

Metamorphosis from pre-war voiturette to post-war Grand Prix car saw the Alfetta grow heavier and wider with extra tankage to meet its ever-mounting thirst. The final version shown here scaled nearly 1800lb, but offset it with a fierce 420bhp and a maximum speed of close on 200mph

BETTI

Power pack: the 1½-litre straight-eight Alfa Romeo engine in its final 1951 high-boost two-stage supercharged form, when it gave over 400 bhp at 9600 rpm

first real defeat in 12 years, when Gonzalez won the British GP at Silverstone for Ferrari.

Two more blows followed swiftly when the newer V12s took the German and Italian GPs, but in a dramatic finale, aided by a Ferrari error in choosing the wrong tyres, Fangio won the Spanish GP in his 159 and with it the second World Championship. Like Germany before the Second World War, the Italian Government at that time paid their premier racing team an annual subsidy, but when Alfa Romeo told them how much they needed for 1952 they said

no. Perhaps Alfa Romeo did not really mind; the day of the small, highly supercharged engine was manifestly over, and they had gone out with a fine flourish. And with a truly grand total of 33 victories, 26 of them achieved in an unbroken row, the *Alfetta* stands as one of the most successful GP cars in history.

Specification
Engine
Eight cylinders, in-line; bore and stroke, 58 × 70 mm; capacity, 1479 cc; twin overhead camshafts operating two valves per cylinder; single Roots-type supercharger up to 1946, then 2-stage; twin Marelli magnetos; maximum power, 180 bhp at 7000 rpm in 1938, rising to 420 bhp at 9600 rpm by 1951.
Transmission
Four-speed gearbox in unit with final drive.
Chassis
Tubular side members; independent front suspension by trailing links and transverse leaf spring; swing rear axles with transverse leaf spring; friction-cum-hydraulic dampers. Lockheed hydraulic brakes. Pirelli tyres.
Dimensions
Wheelbase, 8 ft 2·5 in; front track, 4 ft 2 in; rear track, 4 ft 4 in; dry weight, ranging from 1480 to 1785 lb.
Maximum speed
150 mph in 1938, rising to 195 mph by 1951.

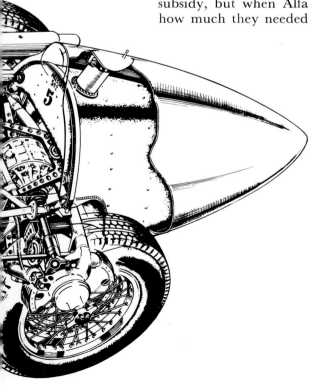

Kurtis-Kraft '3000'

'A man who is no diploma-packing engineer, but who knows his machines with the intimacy that only 35 years of trial-and-error experimentation can give.'

'Motor Trend' on Frank Kurtis

US formula: anticipating the European 'F1 kit car' image by many years, the average American racing car contesting the famous Indianapolis 500 Mile race was built around a proprietary engine and transmission. Kurtis-Kraft of Glendale, California, put theirs together better than most, designed a sturdy chassis embodying many sound and original ideas, and reaped the benefit. This is the 4½-litre Offenhauser-powered Type 3000 with which Johnny Parsons won the 1949 AAA National Championship and the 1950 '500', curtailed to 345 miles by rain. A two-rail tubular truss frame, torsion bar independent front suspension and Halibrand live rear axle are employed, while an aviation-type flexible plastic fuel tank fills the tail

Ever-increasing specialisation at Indianapolis since Miller's 'golden age' opened the gap between European and American motor racing ever wider. The monotonous 2½-mile 'Indy' lap, with its four left-hand banked turns of equal radius, narrowed design needs down to an engine with tremendous upper-end punch and stamina, and a chassis durable enough to withstand 500 miles of punishment at very high speeds. The classic Indianapolis engine is, of course, the immortal Offenhauser which began in 1930 as a Miller unit designed by Leo Goossen, became an Offenhauser in 1936 when Harry Miller's production engineer bought the business, and a Mayer-Drake in 1946 when Lou Meyer and Dale Drake bought out Fred Offenhauser. To Indianapolis faithfuls, however, it remains the fabulous 'Offy', an indestructible 16-valve twin-cam four with five-bearing crankshaft, barrel crankcase, piston speeds exceeding 4000 ft per minute, and an output in the late 1940s of around 280 bhp on carburetters.

These engines could be bought 'over the counter', but with the end of the Miller car in the late 1930s there was no available Indianapolis chassis to fit them into for several years, until the Kurtis-Kraft came along. Frank Kurtis, whose smithy father came from Czechoslovakia, had a plant in Glendale, California, where since 1938 he had built over 800 midget race cars and sundry other interesting vehicles, including Col. J.P. Stapp's unique rocket-propelled sled which attained 632 mph on steel rails (still the fastest manned vehicle on earth) and the notorious Novi Governor Indianapolis specials. With experience like this, building his own track cars was inevitable, but unlike some US designers, Kurtis took heed of European practice.

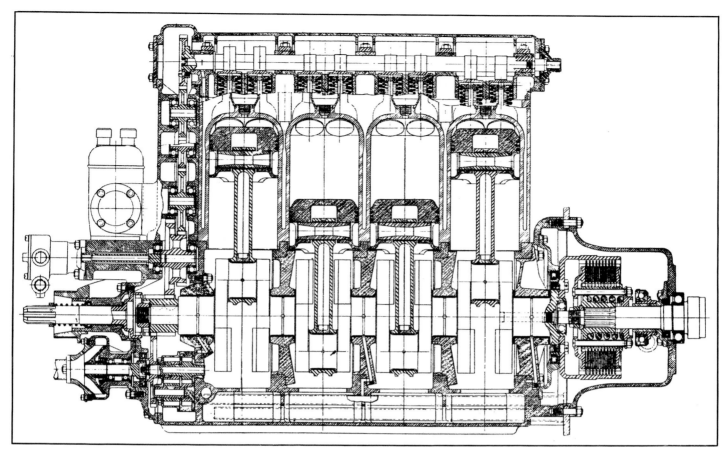

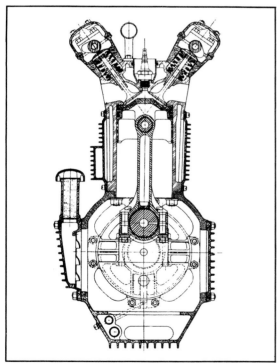

He saw both the 3-litre Maserati 8CTF which introduced torsion bar independent front suspension to Indianapolis, where it sensationally won the 500 in 1939 and 1940, and the 1939 Mercedes-Benz W163 purchased by Don Lee of California, which had de Dion rear suspension. So the first Kurtis-

Kraft '3000' of 1948, sponsored by Ed Walsh, had both torsion bar ifs and a de Dion back end – but both were built with less finesse and greater ruggedness to withstand Indianapolis conditions. Moreover, he was one up on both Maserati and Mercedes with a neat two-rail truss frame of welded 1½in diameter steel tubing, and way ahead with an aircraft-type flexible plastic fuel tank, developed by Firestone and shaped to fill out the entire tail cavity.

His power unit was the faithful 4½-litre (270cu in) Offenhauser, and muscling in on the tough, moneyed Indianapolis track, the first Kurtis '3000' took a modest ninth place after a 25-minute stop. Then the Kurtis-Walsh team took on California midget champion Johnny Parsons to drive the car in AAA National events; he ran second at Milwaukee and Springfield, and won at du Quoin, emerging as runner-up in the 1948 AAA Championship. For 1949 Frank Kurtis replaced the de Dion back end with a Halibrand quick-change axle, still torsion bar sprung, and 'rooky' Parsons shook the Indianapolis establishment by qualifying at a record 132·9mph, then finished second in the 500 itself, and finally won five National Championship races to take the AAA title outright.

By 1950 Kurtis-Kraft Inc. claimed to be

Above: *indefatigable 'Offy': no racing engine can equal the Offenhauser for long and distinguished service; born in 1930, the same basic unit began winning at Indianapolis in 1934 and is still doing so today. This cutaway view of America's famous 16-valve big four in 1951 form as used by Kurtis-Kraft shows the Hillborn-Travers fuel injection, the sturdy five-bearing crankshaft and tubular connecting rods; block and head are a one-piece iron casting*

Left: *end section of the formidable 16-valve Offenhauser engine, as built by Meyer-Drake in 4·2 litre form*

"The Winner" Lee Wallard Indianapolis Motor Speedway -1951-

Lee Wallard in his 1951 Indianapolis-winning Bellanger Special, built by Kurtis-Kraft. A derivative of the 3000, it has slimmer bodywork (albeit marred by an over-generous screen), beam front axle and Halibrand alloy wheels

the 'World's largest manufacturers of racing cars' (though Cooper Cars Ltd might have disagreed), and Parsons in the 'old No. 1' 3000 brought them still more business with an outright victory at Indianapolis, when the 500 was abbreviated by rain to 345 miles, setting new records all the way and averaging 124·002mph. For 1951 an improved '3000' with cleaned up bodywork but the same granite strength underneath was retailed at between $14900 and $20000 according to the engine and equipment fitted. Halibrand pin-drive magnesium wheels, saving 20lb each, became fashionable options, as did Goodyear or Halibrand spot disc brakes. A wholesale switch from carburetters to Hilborn-Travers fuel injection and more potent fuels raised the 'Offy's output to over 300bhp that same year, when Lee Wallard won the Kurtis marque their second 500 Miles victory.

By 1952 engine output had soared to over 330bhp with the aid of methanol and nitro-methane fuels, and the Kurtis-Kraft '3000' was superseded by the highly successful '500' Series, the first of the Indianapolis 'roadsters' with boxed frame, lower build with offset, inclined engine and other changes which brought Kurtis-Kraft three more 'Indy' triumphs in 1953, 1954 and 1955.

Specification
Engine
Meyer-Drake Offenhauser; four cylinders, in-line; bore and stroke, 109·5 × 117·5mm; capacity, 4487cc; twin overhead camshafts operating four valves per cylinder; twin Winfield updraught carburetters; Hunt-Vertex magneto; maximum power, 293bhp at 5000rpm.
Transmission
Two-speed gearbox, propellor shaft, Halibrand final drive.
Chassis
Truss-type tubular frame; independent front suspension by longitudinal torsion bars; Halibrand rigid rear axle with torsion bar suspension. Hydraulic four-wheel drum brakes. Firestone tyres.
Dimensions
Wheelbase, 8ft 4in; dry weight, 1650lb.
Maximum speed
Approximately 155mph.
Variants
Carburetters replaced by Hilborn-Travers fuel injection in 1951; Goodyear or Halibrand spot disc brakes optional in 1951.

Ferrari Type 375

'July 14th was Bastille Day for the Alfa Romeo fortress, successfully stormed by Ferrari.'

'Auto Italiana'

This was the car that deposed the proud Alfa Romeos, kings of Grand Prix racing since 1946. When Commendatore Enzo Ferrari, 18 years with Alfa Romeo before becoming a manufacturer himself, learned that one of his cars had defeated the Type 159s in the 1951 British GP at Silverstone, he said 'I have killed my mother'. He had, in fact, killed the supercharged racing engine. Ferrari loved 12 cylinder engines ever since he saw the US Army staff Packard 'Twin-Sixes' of the First World War, and thus the first Grand Prix Ferraris of 1948 had 1½-litre V12 engines designed by Gioacchino Colombo, whose genius had produced the Type 158 Alfa Romeo. In the idiom of the time, these Ferraris were supercharged, and in the absence of Alfa Romeo in 1949, the new make from Maranello, near Modena, won five Formula 1 races.

With the return of Alfa Romeo in 1950, it was quickly evident that the Ferrari, even with twin-cam heads and two-stage supercharging, was no match for the fierce cars from Portello. Ferrari and his new chief engineer, Aurelio Lampredi, late of Isotta-

Fraschini, had been much impressed by Etancelin's non-stop run into second place in the 312-mile GP of Europe at Monza late in 1949 with a 4½-litre unsupercharged six-cylinder Lago-Talbot. This was achieved by low fuel and tyre consumption and rugged reliability compared with the thirsty and brittle blown cars, and Lampredi argued with Colombo that a lighter, up-to-date chassis with a modern unblown V12 engine could prove a less complicated route to success than that to which Alfa Romeo were committed. Colombo walked out – returning to Alfa, in fact! – and Ferrari bade Lampredi go ahead.

The *Aspirata* ('the unblown'), as they called the resultant 4½-litre Ferrari, was achieved in three stages: a 72 × 68mm 3·3-litre, then an 80 × 68mm 4·1, and, finally, an 80 × 74·5mm, 4494cc unit, mounted in a chassis of rectangular tubing. This had transverse leaf independent front suspension with unequal length wishbones, and a de Dion rear axle, also suspended by a single transverse leaf spring, with Houdaille hydraulic dampers all round. Transmission was through a multi-plate clutch and propellor shaft to a

Aurelio Lampredi's 4½-litre unsupercharged 12-cylinder Ferrari, the car which broke Alfa Romeo's long hold on Grand Prix racing in 1951

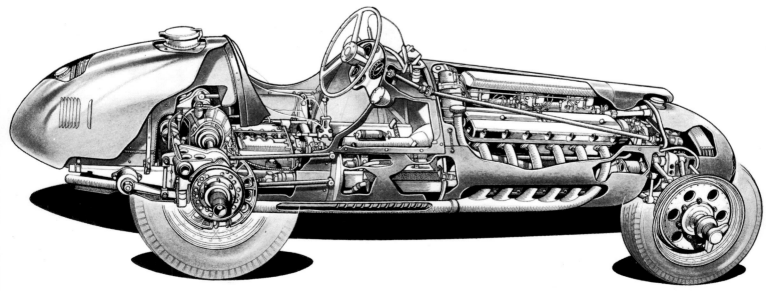

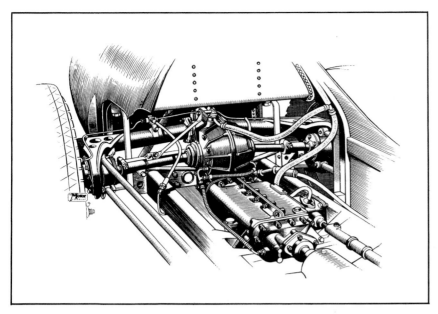

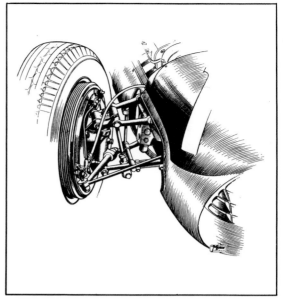

Above: the Type 375 Ferrari four-speed gearbox mounted just ahead of the final drive, with driver's seat above it, to some detriment in frontal area. Chassis side members were of rectangular tube 4·7 in deep; the de Dion-type rear axle was suspended by a single transverse leaf spring, mounted low beneath the frame

Above, right: a transverse leaf spring was also utilised in the 4½-litre Ferrari's independent front suspension, which employed unequal length wishbones and Houdaille hydraulic dampers

Right: Aurelio Lampredi, the ex-Isotta-Fraschini engineer whose 4½-litre V12 Ferrari killed the supercharger in GP racing

four-speed gearbox in unit with the final drive. The engine had its two banks of cylinders at 60 degrees, and there were only single overhead camshafts to each head, driven by one triple roller chain, and operating two valves per cylinder at 60 degrees with hairpin return springs. The cylinder heads and water jackets were a combined alloy casting with 'wet' liners screwed in, and the crankshaft turned in seven Vandervell

'Thin Wall' steel-backed indium-plated bearings. These easily-fitted shell bearings had revolutionised production engine design, and Ferrari was the first to use them in GP racing on his earlier supercharged cars.

The big-end bearings were also of thin-wall type, ignition was by two Marelli magnetos, and there were three Weber twin-choke down-draught carburetters between the blocks, fed with air from a central scoop on the bonnet top, and with a petrol-benzole-alcohol fuel from a 35-gallon rear tank. This large bore/short stroke, relatively simple power unit possessed excellent torque and gave 330 bhp at 6500 rpm in 1950 form, when the cars nosed tentatively onto Alfa territory and, in their absence, scored a warning one-two-three win in the final Penya Rhin GP at Barcelona. With the same cars they took two early 1951 races at Syracuse and Pau, while at San Remo, Ascari won with a boosted version of the 375 having two plugs to each cylinder, raised compression and other engine mods increasing output to 380 bhp at 7500 rpm.

The Cavallino rampante – the prancing horse in Ferrari's badge – and the *Quadrifoglio* of Alfa Romeo first came to grips that decisive year in the Swiss GP, where Ferrari's third string Taruffi split the Alfa Romeo formation to take second place. Two more fighting second placings followed at Spa and Reims, and then came the unforgettable British GP at Silverstone. Froilan Gonzalez, deputising for Taruffi in a 1950 12-plug car, set the first 100 mph lap at Britain's premier circuit during practice, and in the race he scored a magnificent victory over Fangio's Alfa Romeo, aided by a quicker pit stop for less fuel.

Fitted with improved brakes and new built-in perspex windshields in place of the time-honoured folding aero-screen, the *Aspirate* next went to the Nürburgring, where Ascari won the German GP at the 159s' expense; Gonzalez then took an easy Pescara GP with no Alfas running, and Fangio hit back by beating the Ferraris at Bari. The next Championship round, the Italian GP at Monza, saw Ascari win again, with another Ferrari second and the sole surviving Alfa third. The climax to this great inter-Italian battle came in the Spanish GP at Barcelona, where the Ferrari team erred in fitting tyres of too small a diameter. An epidemic of thrown treads cost them the race and enabled Alfa Romeo to bow out of racing on a high note, which perversely pleased the sentimentalist in Enzo Ferrari.

The withdrawal of Alfa Romeo and the poor showing of the V16 BRM caused a wholesale switch to Formula 2 rules for 1952, rendering the Ferrari 375 obsolete just when it had reached full maturity. The cars continued racing in surviving F1 and F.Libre events, both in works and private hands: Villoresi won the 1952 Turin GP and a race at Boreham, Essex; Ascari made an enterprising attempt on the Indianapolis 500 Miles but retired with a broken wheel; Frenchman Louis Rosier acquired a 375 and won the Albi GP both in 1952 and 1953; and in Britain Tony Vandervell, the bearing tycoon, ran two cars as 'Thin Wall Specials', the first a 1950 example which scored firsts at Silverstone, Goodwood and Winfield, Scotland, the second a 1951 24-plug car which was substantially modified between 1952 and 1954, and won several races at Goodwood, Dundrod, Silverstone and elsewhere.

Specification
Engine
V12; bore and stroke, 80 × 74·5mm; capacity, 4494cc; two single overhead camshafts operating 2 valves per cylinder; unsupercharged; 3 Weber twin-choke carburetters; 2 Marelli magnetos and twelve plugs in 1950; twenty-four plugs in 1951; maximum power 330bhp at 6500rpm, rising to 380bhp at 7000 rpm.
Transmission
Four-speed gearbox in unit with final drive.
Chassis
Tubular side members; independent front suspension by wishbones and transverse leaf spring; de Dion rear axle with transverse leaf spring; Houdaille hydraulic dampers. Hydraulic two-leading shoe brakes. Englebert tyres.
Dimensions
Wheelbase, 7ft 7·4in; front track, 4ft 3·5in; rear track, 4ft 3in; dry weight, 1725lb.
Maximum speed
173mph.

José-Froilan Gonzalez, the burly Argentinian who defeated the mighty Alfa Romeos on his second encounter with them in a 4½-litre Ferrari at Silverstone in the 1951 British GP. Here he is on his first Ferrari drive, deputising for Taruffi in the French GP and throwing the car into the tight Thillois turn at Reims in typical forceful style

Mercedes-Benz W196

'So there you are—they're back.'

R. L. Walkerley re. the 1954 French GP in 'The Motor'

Like the W163 of 1939, the Mercedes-Benz W196 of 15 years later was both complex and costly, but achieved its makers' aim of supremacy on the Grand Prix circuits. The straight-eight fuel-injection engine was laid over at 37 degrees from horizontal in the multi-tube space frame to reduce overall height

By proving themselves so good at Grand Prix racing through the years, the old-established firm of Mercedes-Benz gave themselves an extra problem – when they competed they had just *had* to succeed, the world expecting nothing less. After the Second World War, when Germany made such an impressive economic and industrial recovery, racing gossip almost anywhere was periodically enlivened by rumours that the legendary 'Mercs' were returning to racing. Unterturkheim obliged in 1952, but surprised by choosing sports car events: 'We are just opening a little window on the motor racing scene' was how director Fritz Nallinger explained their 300SLs and, as usual, when they raced they won. Then, with a fine sense of the dramatic, they made their Grand Prix comeback in 1954, first year of the new 750cc blown/2500cc unblown Formula, 20 years after their first victory in the 750kg Formula introduced in 1934, and 40 years after their epic 1914 one-two-three Grand Prix triumph.

From every aspect the Mercedes-Benz which lined up for the French GP at Reims on July 4th, 1954, were sensational. Externally, they wore superbly formed, all-enveloping aerodynamic bodies ideally suited to the very fast triangular circuit. Internally they contained surprise after surprise. The chassis was of the then new 'space-frame' type, welded up from thin-diameter tube to form a light but rigid structure wherein all members are either in compression or tension. The engine was not the vee-type one might expect for its compactness and Mercedes' past experience; the design staff, headed by Hans Scherenberg and Rudolf Uhlenhaut, rejected the layout on grounds of excess weight and chose a straight-eight – the last to appear in GP racing apart from an abortive Gordini. Like the 1932 B-type Alfa Romeo, this had central timing gears with a block of four cylinders on each side. Bore and stroke were 76 × 68·8mm (2496cc) and initial power figures of 257bhp at 8200rpm promised some vigorous competition in the new Formula.

Naturally the cylinders were built up in traditional Mercedes style with welded-on ports and water jackets, but this time the twin overhead camshafts operated two large valves only to each cylinder at 90 degrees, the exhausts having sodium-cooled stems. A Hirth built-up crankshaft ran in 10 roller bearings, and the one-piece connecting rods also turned in rollers. There were no valve springs; instead the D–B engineers had perfected a positive 'desmodromic' system employing two cams of diverse forms, one for opening the valves, the other for closing,

aided by gas pressure from the cylinders. Nor were there any carburetters, a Bosch direct fuel injection system, as first developed for the 300SL, taking their place.

Further surprises were the canting-over of the whole engine at 37 degrees from the horizontal (to achieve low frontal area), and the power take-off from the centre of the crankshaft through a sub-shaft (as on the first 16-cylinder BRM), a dry single-plate clutch and a propellor shaft passing under the rear-axle line to a five-speed gearbox with Porsche-type synchromesh on the four top

Upholding an old Mercedes tradition, the W196 won first time out, at Reims in the 1954 French GP, Fangio and Kling finishing half a length apart. Here is the third member of the team, Hans Herrmann, cornering his stromlinien-wagen at Thillois; he made fastest lap at 121·46 mph, but paid for it in smoky retirement

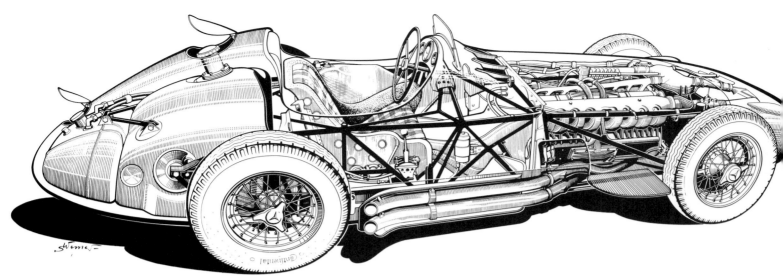

Right-side view of the 2½-litre Mercedes-Benz was less pleasing with the untidy twin exhaust pipes discharging ahead of the rear wheels. The twin overhead camshaft engine with Bosch direct fuel injection and desmodromic valve gear produced about 257 bhp at 8200 rpm in 1954, in a car weighing 1670 lb dry

ratios. This gearbox was integral with the final drive, and swing rear axles with double universal joints were located by two curved arms pivoted to give a low roll centre, the suspension medium being longitudinal torsion bars and finned hydraulic dampers. Finally, the turbo-cooled hydraulic brakes at front and rear were mounted inboard to reduce unsprung weight, those at the front being on jointed half-axles sprung by parallel wishbones and torsion bars.

With a wealth of advanced thought in detail design features, activated by a policy of leaving nothing to chance regardless of complexity or cost, these remarkable cars technologically swamped the Ferrari and Maserati opposition of 1954. At Reims, two of the silver projectiles catapulted to the

front and remained there throughout the 311-mile race, finishing first and second a mere yard apart, but over a lap ahead of the third-placed Ferrari. The third W196 set fastest lap at 121·46mph, but suffered for it with piston failure. Aerodynamic bodywork that paid dividends at Reims did the reverse at Silverstone in the British GP; Fangio could not place his unseen front wheels accurately and, additionally hampered by incorrect tyres and marked understeer, finished fourth with battered corners and only three of his five speeds left. But road-racing bodywork was ready in time for the GP of Europe at the Nürburgring, when the aesthetic beauty of the *stromlinienwagen* gave way to an ugly if purposeful open body, low and squat with a gaping maw at the front and

Open wheeler: Juan Manuel Fangio quickly proved the road racing W196 to be effective if not unduly handsome by winning first time out in the 1954 Grand Prix of Europe at the Nürburgring in Germany

uncouth paired exhausts discharging ahead of the left-hand rear wheel.

If the road-racing W196 was the first less-than-beautiful racing car to come from Unterturkheim, it was Mercedes-Benz all through on performance. In that European GP Fangio won easily; at Berne and Monza he won again; at Barcelona he led until the car broke, but still won the World Championship. And in 1955, aided by 290bhp, the master took the title again, winning the Argentine, Belgian, Dutch and Italian GPs in a season deprived of four Grands Prix because of the Le Mans tragedy. At Aintree, where new team member Stirling Moss won the British GP, the silver cars placed 1–2–3–4, but failure of all three cars at Monaco had prevented complacency and encouraged the opposition.

The Mercedes reputation was enhanced by equal success in the sports car class with the potent 3-litre 300SLR of Formula 1 derivation; these scored five wins in 1955, Stirling Moss taking the major three and securing the World Sports Car Championship. Following this spectacular double triumph, Daimler-Benz surprised the racing world yet again by suddenly announcing their total withdrawal from motor racing at the close of 1955. The cars obviously had great potential for future development (those jointed front half-shafts and inboard brakes inviting four-wheel-drive, for example) but the directors' decision was final. Those believing that Mercedes-Benz plan their spectacular returns to racing every 20 years waited in vain in 1974, but the impact of the 1954–55 seasons, allied to earlier achievements, still endures today.

Specification
Engine
Eight cylinders, in-line; bore and stroke, 76 × 68·8mm; capacity, 2496cc; twin overhead camshafts, desmodromic operation; two valves per cylinder; Bosch direct fuel injection; Bosch magneto; maximum power, 257bhp at 8200rpm, rising to 290bhp at 8500rpm.
Transmission
Five-speed gearbox in unit with final drive.
Chassis
Tubular space frame; independent front suspension by wishbones and torsion bars; swing rear axles with torsion bars; hydraulic dampers. ATE inboard hydraulic brakes. Continental tyres.
Dimensions
Wheelbase, 7ft 8·5in; front track, 4ft 4·4in; rear track, 4ft 5in; dry weight, 1670lb (in 1954), 1607lb (in 1955).
Variants
Wheelbase reduced to 7ft 3in in 1955; special 7ft 0·6in short wheelbase car with outboard front brakes for Monaco 1955.

Totalitarian rule prevailed at Aintree in the 1955 British GP when the Mercedes-Benz team took the first four places in the order Moss, Fangio, Kling, Taruffi, with only five surviving cars behind them from a field of 22 starters. On the front row of the grid are Behra (Maserati No. 2), Fangio and Moss, who won by a fifth of a second from his No. 1

75

Maserati 250F

'It really was a very nice car to drive.'

Stirling Moss

A good designer is always versatile. Having produced a blown 1½-litre straight eight for Alfa Romeo, then a blown V12 for Ferrari, Gioacchino Colombo was called in by Count Orsi of the Officine Alfieri Maserati SpA to improve the performance of their 1952 2-litre six-cylinder Formula 2 car. He fitted dual ignition, raised rpm and output from 175 to 190 bhp, modified the suspension and brakes, and in the resultant A6SSG provided some worthwhile opposition for the Ferraris and Fangio with a winner in the Italian and Modena GPs of 1953. By then Maserati's new 2½-litre 1954 Formula 1 design, the 250F, was well advanced and Colombo's ideas, and those of Ing. Bellentani and Maserati's technical director-to-be Giulio Alfieri, all contributed to this outstanding car.

Its engine followed the basic pattern of the earlier 2-litre unit, but for the remainder the designers were able to employ those features which Colombo earnestly desired but had to

Vitally aided by the uncanny skill of J.M. Fangio, the Maserati 250F enjoyed a brilliant debut to its five-year career, winning first time out at Buenos Aires in the Argentine GP, and again at Spa in the Belgian GP, round two of the 1954 World Championship

forgo owing to the imminent expiry of the 1952–53 Formula 2. The Achilles heel of the Maserati had long been its rigid rear axle with quarter-elliptic leaf springing; now a new de Dion back end was built, unusual in having the beam ahead of the 'transaxle' – i.e., combined final drive and four-speed gearbox, which was of transverse type, and mounted offset. Rear suspension was by a transverse leaf spring above the axle line, front suspension was of 2-litre type by un-equal-length wishbones and coil springs with an anti-roll bar, and the very large hydraulic brakes had finned backplates and ventilated alloy drums giving an extractor effect.

The early post-war type of chassis formed from two large-diameter tubes was now dead, and the 250F had an all-new multi-tubular 'near' – space frame which was both lighter and stiffer. Cylinder dimensions of the straight-six engine were 84 × 75 mm (2493 cc) and the crankshaft ran in seven Vandervell VP thin-wall bearings. There were the

customary twin overhead camshafts operating two valves per cylinder, but these followed the A6SSG in being unequally inclined, the inlets at 36 degrees from vertical, the exhausts at 41 degrees. Twin Marelli magnetos sparked two plugs per cylinder, and carburation was by triple horizontal double-choke Webers, each having flared extension pipes for ram effect. It was a strong, straightforward engine which served admirably to the end of 1957, the output being raised progressively from 240 bhp at 7200 rpm to 270 at 8000 rpm, materially aided by use of nitromethane in its methyl-alcohol diet.

The bodywork was equally straightforward and efficient, having a projecting nose with elliptical radiator intake, initially embodying the famous Trident motif, a wide wrap-around screen of Plexiglass, and a shapely tail enclosing both a 44-gallon fuel tank and a 4·5-gallon oil reservoir. Like Bugatti and Miller, Maserati made cars to sell as well as running their own works team, and between 1954 and 1958 no less than 34 250Fs were built. In those pre-proprietary days that meant engines, transmissions, chassis and most other components were almost all produced in the Maserati factory in Modena, which did its own pattern-making, foundry-work, toolmaking, machining, and engine, chassis and body manufacture.

Costing well under half the German product, the 250F equalled the Mercedes-Benz W196's feat of winning its first Grand Prix. This was the Argentine GP, the opening round of the World Championship, held in January 1954 and appropriately won by Fangio in the one 250F prepared in time. He also took the second round, the Belgian GP at Spa, before transferring to Mercedes-Benz, the 'Trident' thereby contributing vitally to his second Championship title. Meantime, private owners were receiving their cars, Stirling Moss giving early notice of a strong new combination by winning the Aintree 200, the Oulton Park Gold Cup, Goodwood Trophy and other British events that first year, while Roy Salvadori in a 250F run by Syd Greene also scored numerous home successes up to 1956.

Space limitations prevent a full record of all 250F achievements (indeed, the cars are still winning regularly in historic racing car events) but suffice it to say that they scored over 40 race wins, these including six important F1 events in 1954, five in 1955, four in 1956 (among them the Monaco and Italian GPs by Stirling Moss in works cars) and seven in 1957, their golden year, including the Argentine, Monaco, French and German GPs by Fangio while winning his fifth World Champion title.

By then the car had developed from its slightly portly 1954 form into a wickedly handsome machine with lightened chassis, five speeds, improved and still more copiously ventilated brakes, a long, sleek nose and an impressively riveted tail. Financial straits aggravated by an over-ambitious sports car racing programme cut short the Maserati 250F's career at the end of 1957; many continued racing, and Fangio drove his last

British driver Stirling Moss winning a model Monaco GP victory in 1956. He led in the works 250F Maserati from flag fall, despite every effort by Fangio to catch him with first one, then another Lancia-Ferrari

Fangio, back in a 250F after three seasons, scored the greatest of all his many great victories in the 1957 German Grand Prix at Nürburgring, when in defeating the Ferraris he broke the lap record ten times. The car had slimmed considerably since 1954 although power from its 2½-litre six-cylinder engine rose by only 30bhp in four seasons

race in the 1958 French GP with a modified short-wheelbase car. By then the 250F was eclipsed both by the compatriot Ferrari V6s and the British Vanwalls, but it will always remain a classic example of the front-engined Formula 1 car, one remembered with great affection by two masters who raced it, Fangio and Moss, for its ever-willing performance and superbly balanced and responsive handling.

Specification
Engine
Six cylinders, in-line; bore and stroke, 84 × 75mm; capacity, 2493cc; twin overhead camshafts operating two valves per cylinder; three down-draught Weber carburetters; twin Marelli magnetos, and two plugs per cylinder; maximum power, 240bhp at 7200rpm, rising to 270bhp at 8000rpm.

Transmission
Four-speed transverse gearbox in 1954; five-speed box in 1955-57, in unit with final drive.

Chassis
Multi-tubular space frame; front suspension by wishbones and coil springs; de Dion type rear axle with transverse leaf spring; Houdaille hydraulic dampers. Hydraulic two-leading shoe drum brakes. Pirelli tyres (works cars).

Dimensions
Wheelbase, 7ft 5·75in; front track, 4ft 3in; rear track, 4ft 1·25in; dry weight, 1386lb.

Lancia-Ferrari V8

'. . . this King of the 1956 Grand Prix cars.'

Paul Frère

In 1899 a young apprentice named Vincenzo Lancia worked as clerk, mechanic and tester in Giovanni Ceirano's motor works in Turin. The works were acquired by a big new company, FIAT, and Lancia went with them. Such was his talent at the wheel that they made him a racing driver, and although most FIAT victories fell to his polished colleague Nazarro, Vincenzo the pacemaker generally broke the lap record before breaking his car. His keen mechanical bent soon sent Lancia in a new direction, building cars of his own. Automobili Lancia, born 1906, was soon going strong, but its founder firmly eschewed motor racing; he knew its lure too well and would not involve his firm in the heavy costs.

Vincenzo Lancia had a son, Gianni, who inherited his father's love for racing cars, and became managing director of the company after the Second World War. Soon special versions of the road Aurelia were racing, followed by a special V6 sports-racing car, the D24, which gained many big wins in 1953. But Gianni's ambition went further, and by 1954 a Grand Prix Lancia was on the way. The great Vittorio Jano was designer,

and ace drivers Ascari and Villoresi were signed up at great cost long before the cars were ready. Not until the final race of 1954, the GP of Spain at Barcelona, did the new D50 make its debut, but then the waiting seemed worthwhile; Ascari was fastest in practice, passed the Mercedes and led the race from laps three to nine, and made fastest lap before retiring with clutch trouble.

Jano and the Lancia engineers worked busily that winter preparing for 1955. It was a bold design, attractively small, short, low and light in contrast with its rivals. The engine was a four-camshaft 73·6 × 73·1 mm 90 degree V8, the first specifically designed to serve as a stressed member in a tubular space-frame. Cast-in lugs at the four corners of the unit bolted to the front and central tubular bulkheads, with linking tubes lower down. Springing all round was by transverse leaf springs, with a de Dion beam at the rear and an independent front end with double wishbone links, the upper ones having rocker extensions to inboard tubular dampers. The engine was *desaxé* in the frame, the angled propellor shaft running through drop gears left of the driver's seat to a hydraulic-

An unexpected visitor to Britain in 1955 was an original V8 Lancia D50, sent over for Mike Hawthorn to drive in the Oulton Park Gold Cup race. He finished second to Moss's Maserati

Above: *Alberto Ascari about to try out the prototype D50 Lancia, still unpainted. The desaxé-mounted V8 engine, side fuel tanks and general compact build can be seen*

Above, right: *the handover: six complete D50 Grand Prix cars and two extra bodies lined up at Turin for the official passing of all Lancia Formula 1 racing material to the Scuderia Ferrari in mid-1955*

ally operated clutch in the final drive housing, transmitting to an integral five-speed transverse gearbox.

The major external surprise was the use of separate, pannier-type fuel tanks located on faired outriggers between the wheels, Jano's objectives being unchanging weight distribution as the fuel emptied and improved airflow between the wheels. Output for the V8 engine was quoted at 260 bhp at 8200 rpm, comparing with the initial 257 bhp of the rival Mercedes-Benz, while the D50 was over 280 lb lighter, giving promise of some exciting racing in 1955. In the opening GP in Argentina, however, the short, light cars revealed alarming tendencies to sudden breakaway, and although drivers Ascari, Villoresi and Castellotti bickered briefly for the lead, all three retired. Ascari salved Lancia pride somewhat a few weeks later by beating the Maseratis and Ferraris to win the Turin GP on home ground. Then he lost to Maserati at Pau through brake trouble, but offset it with another win in the Naples GP.

Then came the dramatic Monaco GP, where Ascari inherited the lead after the last of the Mercedes broke down, only to skid off-course and plunge straight into the harbour. Four days later Ascari was killed when trying out a sports Ferrari at Monza, and the spine went out of Lancia's racing effort just when they were becoming a power in the land. At the same time dire financial troubles in the Lancia business fabric came to a head; Gianni Lancia's heavy expen-

diture on racing was partly to blame, and the Lancia family sold out their interests to a powerful outside group, who promptly called a halt to the Formula 1 programme.

Meanwhile Scuderia Ferrari had struck a bad patch. The Lampredi-designed 2-litre fours which dominated the 1952–53 seasons had been enlarged to 2½ litres and improved for 1954, but were hard pressed to keep up with the opposition. Enzo Ferrari let it be known that his famous stable was in need of support if it was to continue, and on July 7th, 1955, he was surprised to learn that, through the combined efforts of Fiat, the AC d'Italia and the ANFIAA (Italy's equivalent of the SMMT) the new Lancia directors had agreed to hand over all their F1 material to Ferrari, while Fiat would contribute an annual sum of 50 million lire (about £28,500) for a period of five years.

At a stroke, therefore, Ferrari inherited six racing cars, designer Vittorio Jano, several transporters and other material. While the gift was assimilated the Lancia D50s raced but twice, at Spa where Castellotti lay third but retired, and at Oulton Park, England, where Mike Hawthorn took second place in the Gold Cup race. During the off-season sundry permutations of Ferrari and Lancia parts were tried out before the official 1956 team cars emerged as modified D50s. An extra 12 bhp was extracted from the engines, but Jano's enterprising stress-sharing idea was scrapped, as were his side tanks, the empty panniers remaining, now bridged

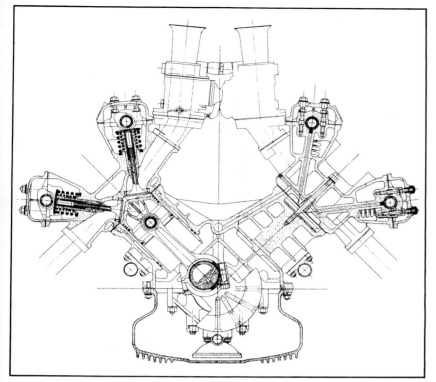

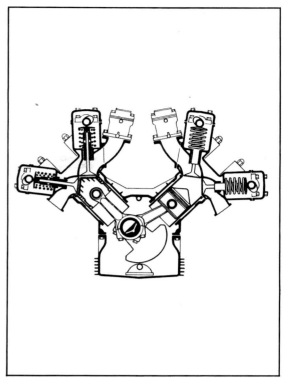

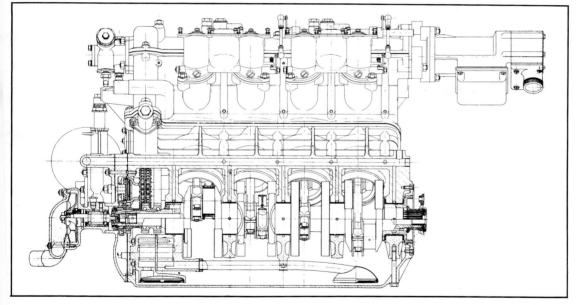

Above, left: *end section of the Lancia V8 D50 engine as initially modified by Ferrari. Coil valve return springs and direct-acting cams have replaced the hairpin valve springs and cam followers originally prescribed by Vittorio Jano*

Above: *the Ferrari-built version as raced in 1957 has an all-new block, modified port angles for the four Solex double-choke carburetters, and other refinements. The integrally-cast tube mountings each side of the cylinder blocks have disappeared*

Left: *side elevation of the engine, originally designed as a stressed member within the multi-tubular chassis*

solidly to the body and the exhaust pipes discharging through them. Fuel was now carried in normal tail tanks, where its weight improved 'feel' and made the cars more manageable. With these, plus one other invaluable asset, Juan Manuel Fangio, Scuderia Ferrari faced the 1956 season.

Things began promisingly with Fangio and Musso sharing first place in the Argentine GP, and Fangio collecting two non-Championship races at Mendoza, in Argentina, and at Syracuse. Then came setbacks; the Lancia/Ferraris lost to Gordini at Naples, to Vanwall at Silverstone, and to Maserati at Monaco. But the British member of the team,

Peter Collins, then won the Belgian GP, and won again in the French GP, where modified, Ferrari-built engines measuring 76 × 68·5 mm and worth several extra bhp were fitted. In the British GP it was Fangio's turn to win, and as the master of the Nürburgring he not unnaturally added the German GP to his bag. In the final Championship round at Monza, marked by an epidemic of tyre, steering and suspension failures on the rough track, Fangio's car broke a steering arm when lying second, whereupon Collins sportingly handed over his own car, enabling the Argentinian to finish second and win his fourth World Champion title.

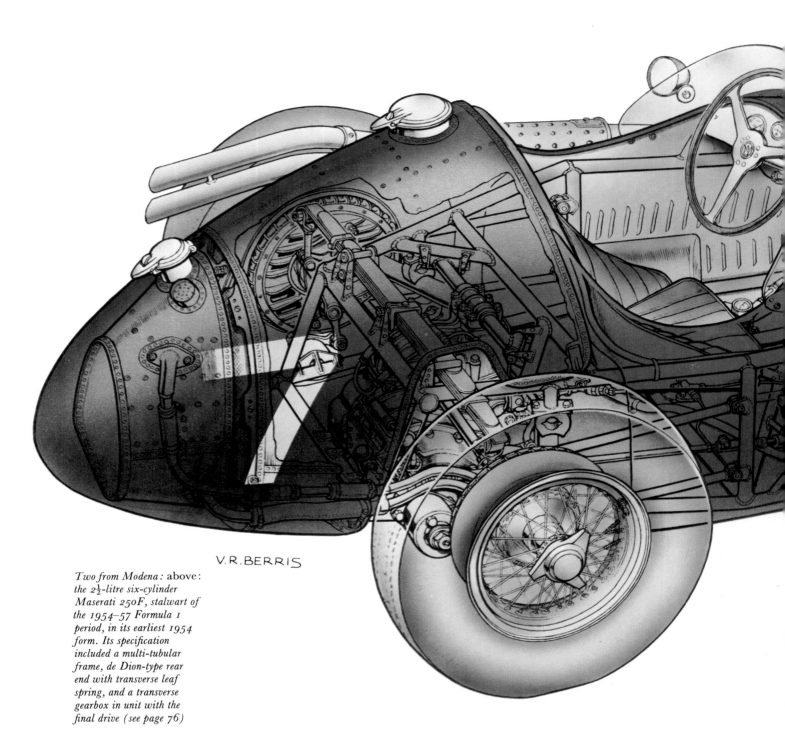

V.R. BERRIS

Two from Modena: above: the 2½-litre six-cylinder Maserati 250F, stalwart of the 1954–57 Formula 1 period, in its earliest 1954 form. Its specification included a multi-tubular frame, de Dion-type rear end with transverse leaf spring, and a transverse gearbox in unit with the final drive (see page 76)

Right: *the 4½-litre unsupercharged V12 Ferrari Type 375 (see page 69) in its final 1952 form, with driver's head fairing and enlarged nose, as prepared for that year's Indianapolis 500 Miles Race. Driver here is Carroll Shelby, giving this historic car an airing at Long Beach in 1976*

82

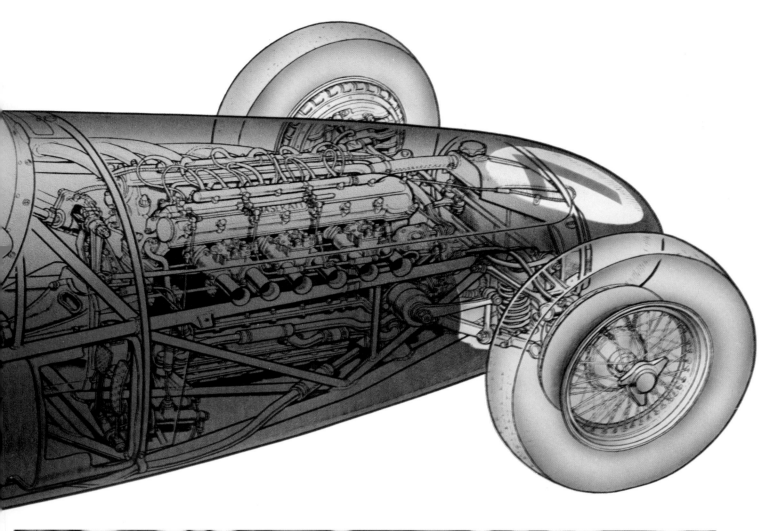

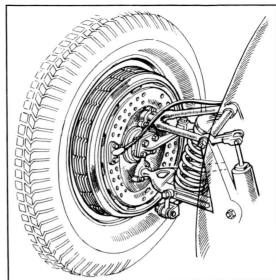

Seemingly eager to erase all vestiges of Lancia ancestry from the one-time D50s, Ferrari removed the side sponsons entirely for the 1957 European season, fitting slim, long-nosed bodywork; they also built new chassis with larger diameter bottom tubes and slightly longer wheelbase, and replaced the front transverse leaf by coil springs. But they lost Fangio to Maserati, and their overall score for the year was depressing; two wins by Collins at Syracuse and Naples, and one by Musso at Reims, all non-Championship events. Clearly it had been Maserati's and Vanwall's season, and at its close the unforgettably raucous blast from the Lancia/ Ferraris was silenced, and the cars were stripped and left to moulder in a shed at Maranello.

Specification
Engine
90 degree V8; bore and stroke, $73 \cdot 6 \times 73 \cdot 1$ mm; capacity, 2489cc in 1954–55; $76 \times 68 \cdot 5$ mm, 2490cc in 1956–57. Four overhead camshafts operating two valves per cylinder; four Solex down-draught twin-choke carburetters; two Marelli magnetos, two plugs per cylinder; maximum power 260bhp at 8200rpm in 1954, rising to 285bhp at 8500rpm in 1957.
Transmission
Five-speed transverse gearbox in unit with final drive
Chassis
Small-diameter tubular space frame; front suspension by double wishbones and transverse leaf spring (1954–56), coil springs in 1957; rear suspension of de Dion type with transverse leaf spring; telescopic hydraulic dampers in 1954, Houdaille vane-type dampers in 1955–57. Hydraulic two-leading shoe drum brakes. Pirelli tyres in 1954, Englebert in 1955–57.
Dimensions
Wheelbase, 7ft 6in in 1954–56, 7ft 8·5in in 1957; track, 4ft 2in, front and rear; dry weight, 1364lb in 1954, 1420lb in 1955–56, 1440lb in 1957.

2½-litre Vanwall

'At last we had got a crack-a-jack Grand Prix car.'

Stirling Moss

When Raymond Mays announced the BRM project in 1946, Britain had been odd man out in Grand Prix racing for a very long time – 22 years in fact, which may surprise those who take the achievements of Cooper, Lotus, McLaren, Tyrrell and others very much for granted in recent years. Not since 1924 had a British car won a Continental Grand Prix, and even then Segrave's supercharged Sunbeam which scored at San Sebastian was embarrassingly 'Fiat' in concept. For patriotic British drivers such as Campbell, Birkin, Howe, Seaman and innumerable race followers it was a galling situation, and continued to be so as the hapless BRM venture, overambitious and underfinanced, floundered on from crisis to crisis into the 1950s.

One influential person who viewed, marked and disapproved its endeavours from the inside was G.A. (Tony) Vandervell, maker of the VP Thin Wall engine bearings which the Italians were very happy to use from 1948. He had willingly joined the BRM board of consultant directors, offering his company's facilities in 1946, but by 1950, disillusioned by the lack of results, this gruff,

strong-minded, dedicated man resigned and set out to create his own British racing team. Up to 1954 he ran ex-works Ferraris as 'Thin Wall Specials', initially the blown 1½-litre V12s, then the big, unblown 4½-litre cars, which were much improved with disc brakes and other modifications, won many British Formule Libre races, and gave the Acton team invaluable experience.

Late in 1952 Tony Vandervell began building his own Grand Prix car, with a 2-litre power unit virtually comprising four 500cc twin overhead camshaft Norton racing motorcycle engine top ends and internals, but watercooled and fitted to a special crankcase adapted from a Rolls-Royce B40 engine designed for military use. Being a director of Norton Motorcycles Ltd helped vitally here, but the first Vanwall Special was not ready for racing until 1954, when Formula 2 had expired and the new 2½-litre Formula 1 was in force. The car had a tubular frame built by Cooper Cars Ltd of Surbiton, using suspension of basic Ferrari pattern (coil spring independent at the front and a de Dion back end with transverse leaf spring). Goodyear disc brakes, as developed for the last Thin

The new look: Although high-built, the Costin-bodied 2½-litre Vanwall brought new aerodynamic standards to Formula 1 with its low-penetration nose, smooth low-drag body with no projections, and full-length undershield. Stirling Moss won first time out with the car in the 1956 International Trophy race at Silverstone

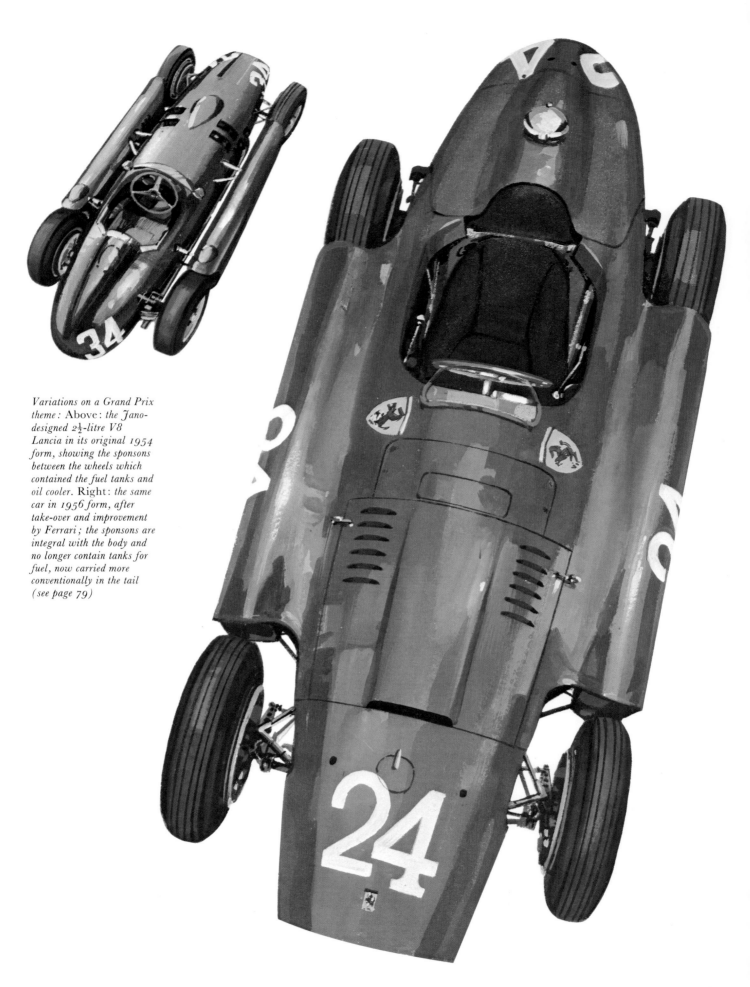

Variations on a Grand Prix
theme: Above: the Jano-
designed 2½-litre V8
Lancia in its original 1954
form, showing the sponsons
between the wheels which
contained the fuel tanks and
oil cooler. Right: the same
car in 1956 form, after
take-over and improvement
by Ferrari; the sponsons are
integral with the body and
no longer contain tanks for
fuel, now carried more
conventionally in the tail
(see page 79)

Right and below: *the
superbly streamlined
Mercedes-Benz 2½-litre
straight-eight W196 of
1954–55 (see page 72),
with full-width aerodynamic
bodywork as successfully
employed at Reims, Monza
and Avus. Bottom: This is
basically the same car with
open-wheeled road racing
body, in the form with
which Stirling Moss headed
a Mercedes 1–2–3–4
victory parade in the 1955
British GP at Aintree*

At a time of six-, eight- and
12-cylinder engines,
Vanwall's Norton-based
2½-litre fours seemed
retrogressive – until they
found their form. Ken
Wharton's 1955 car is
seen here at Monza in
practice for the Italian GP

Cutaway drawing showing
disposition of the main
components in the 2½-litre
Formula 1 Vanwall, the car
which put Britain back on
the Grand Prix map by
winning three GPs in 1957
and six in 1958, when it
was awarded the first
World Manufacturers'
Championship title. Its
specification included
'oversquare' four-cylinder
twin-cam engine with
sodium-cooled valves and
fuel injection, five-speed
gearbox combined with the
final drive, disc brakes all
round, inboard at the rear,
and tubular space frame

Wall Specials, were an advanced feature
when the Continentals still used drums.

The first engine measured 86 × 86 mm
(1998 cc), giving 235 bhp at 7500 rpm. It was
unusual in having the two overhead camshafts carried each in a separate housing on
pedestals, the valve stems and hairpin
return springs being conveniently exposed
for cooling. The exhaust valves were sodium-
cooled, ignition was by BTH magneto and
two plugs per cylinder, and there were four
Amal motorcycle-type carburetters. The
crankshaft naturally turned in VP Thin Wall
bearings – four at first, later five; a five-speed
gearbox was integral with the final drive, and
the green-painted Ferrari-like body carried
an unusual surface radiator on its nose. The
Vanwall's first race was the 1954 International Trophy at Silverstone, where Alan
Brown lay fifth in the final behind four 2½-
litre F1 cars when an oil-pipe broke. From
then until 1956 were the formative years for
Vandervell's ambition.

The engine had been enlarged to 2·3 litres
and a normal radiator fitted when Peter
Collins drove the car, first in the British GP
when he retired, and then in its first Continental race, the Italian GP, finishing
seventh. The Vanwall became a full 2½-litre
(96 × 86 mm, 2490 cc) in time to score two
second places to Stirling Moss's 250F Maserati at Goodwood and Aintree, and then was
fitted with Bosch fuel injection in time for
1955. That was a Mercedes year, of course,

and with Ferrari, Maserati and Lancia all
present the new British interlopers had a lean
time, being dogged by various troubles in the
major Grands Prix. Four minor home wins at
Crystal Palace, Snetterton and Castle Combe
were mild encouragement, and major improvements were put in hand that winter.

Engine breathing specialist Harry Weslake
co-operated in development of a new cylinder
head, the de Dion axle was modified, and the
five-speed gearbox was improved with
Porsche-type synchromesh, but the most
radical changes were in the chassis and body.
Colin Chapman, whose Lotus concern then
was still concentrating on the small sports car
classes, was hired to design a new and proper
space frame, and his colleague Frank Costin
produced a sensationally-formed body which
compensated for the Vanwall's rather high
build by its smooth, drag-free surfaces, flush
fastenings, NACA-type sunken air ducts, re-
cessed exhaust manifold, and complete nose-
to-tail undershielding. Overall the car
weighed just over 1690 lb laden, and with
280 bhp, the Vanwall was emerging as the
most serious British attempt for years in
Grand Prix racing, with a determined patron,
a completely professional team at Acton, and
toolroom, manufacturing and testing facilities
bordering on Mercedes-Benz standards of
thoroughness.

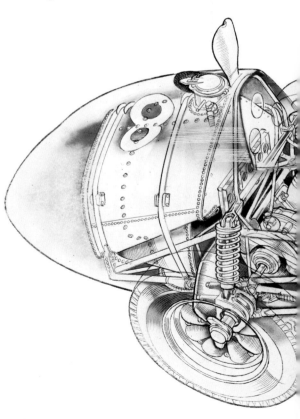

Yet, following an intoxicating first victory in the 180-mile Silverstone International Trophy by 'guest driver' Moss, 1956 proved extremely disappointing for Vanwall apart from some spirited 'mixing it' by Harry Schell in the French GP, when he got amidst the leading Ferraris and showed the Vanwall's formidable pace. More off-season improvements included the replacement of the de Dion rear end leaf springing by coil springs and coaxial telescopic hydraulic dampers, and use of a new fuel mix which raised output to 285 bhp at 7300 rpm. Vandervell then signed up Stirling Moss, Tony Brooks and Stuart Lewis-Evans as an all-British driver team for 1957, Moss losing the season's first race at Syracuse, Sicily, because of a broken injection pipe. This was due to vibration from the big four-cylinder engine, and four more races were to pass

Above, left: *Rouen, 1957, with the Vanwall team awaiting practice for the French GP. Roy Salvadori is in number 20, and Stuart Lewis-Evans's car is behind*

Above: *Monaco, 1957, and Tony Brooks takes the Gasometer hairpin during his drive to second place in the GP behind Fangio. The Vanwall wore a special short nose to avoid contact with other cars on the crowded round-the-houses circuit*

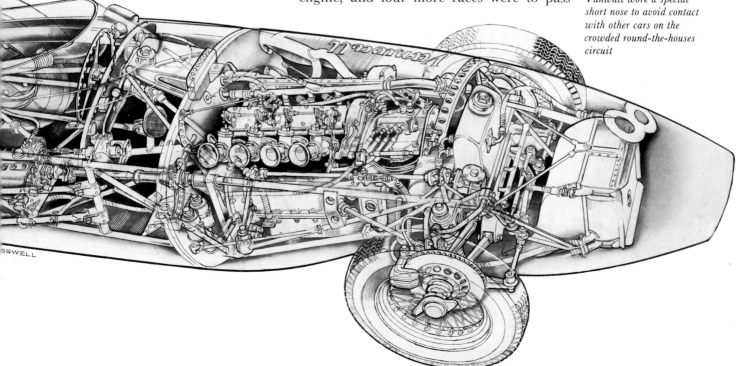

$1\frac{1}{2}$ Litres: despite initial unpopularity, particularly in Britain, the $1\frac{1}{2}$-litre Formula 1 of 1961–65 produced some interesting design variants and brought new marques and nations into Grand Prix racing

Right: the famous Honda motorcycle concern brought Japan on the scene with the technically stimulating transverse V12-engined car, seen here in the 1965 Belgian GP at Spa, driven by the Californian Richie Ginther. He finished sixth, but at the close of that season scored an impressive victory in the Mexican GP (see page 109)

Below: Porsche of Zuffenhausen brought Germany back to Formula 1 in 1962 with a two-car team of flat-eights driven by Dan Gurney and Joakim Bonnier. The latter is seen at Aintree during the 1962 British GP before his retirement with transmission trouble (see page 104)

Below: *the most successful BRM in a quarter-century was the 1½-litre V8 (see page 101) with which Graham Hill won the World Drivers' Championship in 1962 after victories in the Dutch, German, Italian and South African GPs*

before the problem was mastered and the bad spell ended.

The break for which Vandervell and Britain had waited so long came at Aintree when Moss and Brooks jointly won the European GP ahead of three Ferraris. Moss went on to take the Pescara and Italian GPs in the very 'lion's den' of the opposition, each time heading Fangio's Maserati, and when Maserati withdrew in 1958, Formula 1 became largely a Vanwall v Ferrari battle-ground, with the little rear-engined Coopers nosing in. At a loss of about 17 bhp the Vanwalls had been converted to run on the obligatory Avgas fuel, but the GP races were shortened that year from 300 to around 200 miles, meaning less weight of fuel to carry. Light alloy 'wobbly web' wheels were fitted, and with subtle weight-saving elsewhere overall performance did not materially suffer.

In a season euphoric for British green, Moss won the Dutch, Portuguese and Moroccan Grands Prix, and Brooks won the Belgian, German and Italian, Vanwall emerging as winners of the first World Manufacturers' Championship. It had been a long, hard fight to the top, which quite exhausted the single-minded Tony Vander-

vell; on medical advice he reluctantly disbanded his beloved Formula 1 team, and sadly the beautiful green Vanwalls disappeared from the circuits.

Specification
Engine
Four cylinders, in-line; bore and stroke, 96 × 86 mm; capacity, 2490 cc; twin overhead camshafts operating two valves per cylinder; Bosch fuel injection; BTH magneto; maximum power, 285 bhp at 7300 rpm.
Transmission
Five-speed gearbox in unit with final drive.
Chassis
Tubular space frame; front suspension by wishbones and coil springs; de Dion rear suspension with coil springs. Fichtel & Sachs hydraulic dampers. Vandervell-Goodyear disc brakes, inboard at rear. Pirelli tyres (1954-57); Dunlop tyres (1958).
Dimensions
Wheelbase, 7 ft 6·25 in; front track, 4 ft 5·75 in; rear track, 4 ft 3·75 in; dry weight, 1375 lb.

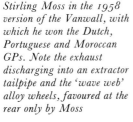

Stirling Moss in the 1958 version of the Vanwall, with which he won the Dutch, Portuguese and Moroccan GPs. Note the exhaust discharging into an extractor tailpipe and the 'wave web' alloy wheels, favoured at the rear only by Moss

Ferrari Dino 246

'The new car is good looking.'

'Autocourse'

'With its long snout and winding exhausts the new Ferrari is ugly.'

'Sports Cars Illustrated'

Automobili Ferrari of Maranello have given Formula 1 racing consistently greater support than any other make in the world, from its inception in 1948 to the present day. The colourful red cars have for so long been an essential part of motor racing that it is difficult to realise that at one stage the proud Comm. Enzo Ferrari was doing so badly that he had to make a public appeal for support. That was in 1955, when Mercedes-Benz won five Grands Prix and Ferrari just one. His appeal brought a five-year annual subsidy of 50 million lire from Fiat, and the handing over, lock, stock and barrel, of the Lancia Formula 1 team, broken by financial dramas behind the scenes and the death of their number one driver, the great Alberto Ascari. Vittorio Jano himself, artificer of the immortal Type B Monoposto Alfa Romeo in 1932 and designer of the F1 Lancia D50, came with the deal, and under Ferrari he made the car into a 1956 winner, Fangio scoring five victories and his fourth World Championship, and Peter Collins winning two Grands Prix.

In 1957 the Maseratis and Vanwalls were too good, and Ferrari's F1 share was meagre, but fortunately they had a promising reserve in an exceptional 1½-litre V6, a kind of 'little Lancia' built for Formula 2 racing. Coming from a long sojourn with Lancia, for whom he had produced the outstanding Aurelia V6 engine, Jano laid this Ferrari design down in 1956. Its cylinders measured 70 × 64·5mm, and were in two staggered banks of three, cast in one unit with the crankcase at 65 degrees; there were four overhead camshafts, two per bank, two plugs per cylinder sparked by magneto, and triple Weber carburetters, all contributing to about 165bhp. The engine was mounted *desaxé* in a tubular frame and drove through a four-speed gearbox integral with the rear axle. Preoccupation with the flagging 1957 F1 cars meant this pretty F2 was used too rarely, but Musso took the 1½-litre class of the Naples GP and Trintignant won the Reims F2 race after a hard struggle with the Cooper-Climaxes.

The car was designed from the start to run on pump fuel, and the Maranello works took the exploratory step of enlarging the V6 engine, first to 1860cc for the 1957 Modena GP where they placed a promising second and fourth, then to 2417cc for the Casablanca

By winning the French GP at Reims, where he averaged a record 125·46mph, and scoring good placings elsewhere, Mike Hawthorn became World Champion in 1958 with the compact 2½-litre V6-engined Dino Ferrari

Built in Britain, but bearing the colours of the USA and Australia respectively, the Eagle-Weslake V12 (right) and the Repco-Brabham V8 (below) greatly enlivened the opening phase of the 3-litre Formula 1 introduced in 1966. Dan Gurney, kingpin of the Eagle venture (see page 118) won the 1967 Belgian GP at Spa, then led the German GP at Nürburgring to the penultimate lap when a broken half-shaft cost him a second classic win. He is seen here in the Weslake V12-engined car on the Karussel banked turn while leading

Left: *New Zealander Denny Hulme in the V8 Repco-engined Brabham BT20 (see page 115), winning the Monaco GP of 1967, the year he won the World Championship*

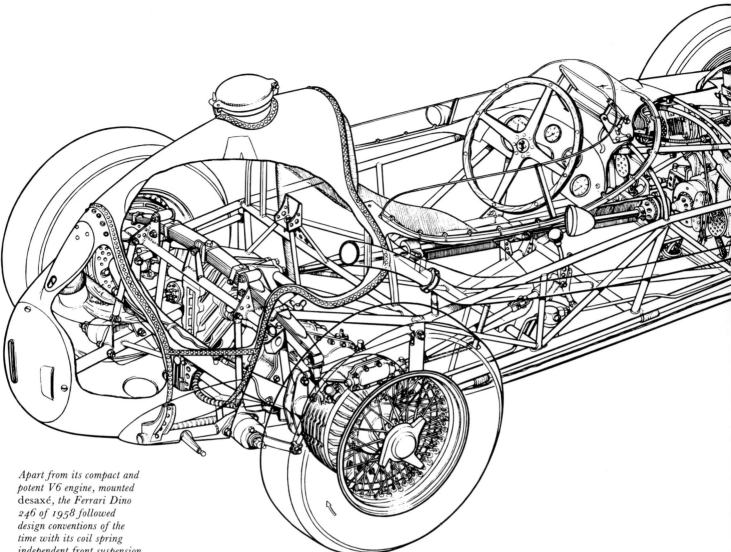

Apart from its compact and potent V6 engine, mounted desaxé, the Ferrari Dino 246 of 1958 followed design conventions of the time with its coil spring independent front suspension, tubular space frame, de Dion back end, and drum brakes in wire wheels

GP. Carrying a third less pump fuel than his nitro-nourished rivals, Collins led for seven laps before retiring after a crash, and Ferrari's vision seemed well rewarded when the FIA confirmed that Formula 1 cars for 1958 must run on 130 octane Avgas commercial fuel instead of their former alcoholic mixtures. So a team of 2½-litre V6 Ferraris was built, the car bearing the name Dino after Enzo Ferrari's son who had died in mid-1957, and the type number 246 for 2·4 litres, 6 cylinders.

Apart from the compact new engine configuration the rest of the car followed normal F1 practice of the time. A new space frame was used, with coil-and-wishbone front springing as on the 1957 Lancia-Ferraris, and a de Dion back end suspended by a single transverse leaf spring. Bore and stroke were 85 × 71 mm, and the punchy engine produced about 275 bhp at 8500 rpm, which compared favourably with the 265 bhp of the first 'Avgas' Vanwall and made the rival 1·9-litre Cooper-Climax's possible 180 bhp seem pitiful. But a harsh lesson was

in store for Ferrari. At 1265 lb dry the Dino was light, but not light enough, and the skimpy little rear-engined Cooper out-handled and out-braked them. By both skill and guile Stirling Moss beat Musso's Dino by 2·7 seconds in the Argentine GP, while Trintignant's similar Cooper won at Monaco from Musso and Collins.

On less serpentine courses the Ferrari drivers could make better use of their cars' potential; Mike Hawthorn won the Goodwood 100 Miles at Easter, Peter Collins did likewise in the International Trophy at Silverstone, while Musso added the Syracuse GP to the list. At Spa they were beaten by Vanwall, but in the French GP at Reims Hawthorn showed the Dino's teeth by beating Moss's Vanwall at a record 125·4 mph. The British GP at Silverstone followed, falling to Collins in masterful style, but this fine driver lost his life in the German GP, after which Maranello morale waned. They won no more Grands Prix that year, but three second placings by Hawthorn secured him

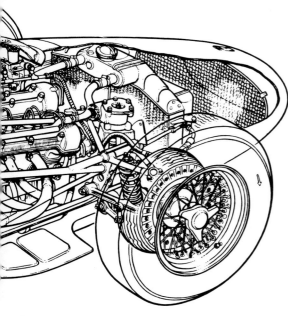

the 1958 World Championship title.

For 1959 an improved Dino appeared. The engine now gave around 280bhp at 8500rpm, there were five speeds instead of four, a new independent back end with co-axial coil spring/hydraulic damper suspension units, Dunlop disc brakes, cleaner but heavier-looking bodywork and a tidier exhaust system. In this car Tony Brooks won both the French and German GPs while Behra won the Aintree 200 Miles, but in other 1959 events it was becoming increasingly clear that the day of the front-mounted engine in Grands Prix was almost done. Phil Hill's rather hollow win with a Dino in the 1960 GP of Europe at Monza, with all the British contenders abstaining, was the very

last Grand Prix victory for a front-engined car. Although traditionalist Enzo Ferrari made the change as reluctantly as he adopted disc brakes, he lost no time once committed, and rear-engined descendants of the 246 were soon bearing the famous 'prancing horse' to another World Championship in 1961.

Specification
Engine
V6; bore and stroke, 85 × 71mm; capacity 2417cc; four overhead camshafts, two valves per cylinder; three twin-choke Weber carburetters; Marelli dual magneto ignition; maximum power, 275bhp at 8500rpm, in 1958, rising to ca. 280bhp in 1959.
Transmission
Four-speed gearbox (five-speed in 1975) in unit with rear final drive.
Chassis
Tubular space frame; wishbones/coil-spring front suspension with anti-roll bar; de Dion rear with transverse leaf spring; Houdaille dampers in 1958, then Koni coaxial telescopic dampers. Hydraulic drum brakes in 1958, Dunlop disc brakes in 1959–60. Englebert tyres.
Dimensions
Wheelbase, 7ft 3·5in; front track, 4ft; rear track, 3ft 11in; dry weight, 1265lb.
Variants
Rear suspension changed to independent by coaxial coil spring telescopic damper units in 1959.

Ferrari's Dino 246 lasted until 1960, being the last serious GP contender with front-mounted engine. Californian driver Phil Hill finished third at Monaco in a car considerably cleaned up in appearance, while he also won the GP of Europe that year

2½-litre Cooper-Climax

'With only 1/27th of Mercedes manpower they (Cooper) won 11 out of 14 races in which they ran . . .'

Laurence E. Pomeroy

The final three years of the 2½-litre Formula 1 became increasingly embarrassing for established GP manufacturers. In 1958 a 'little bumped-up Cooper 500', costing a fraction of their sophisticated creations, pushed in and won two Championship Grands Prix; in 1959 it won five and took the World Drivers' and Manufacturers' Championships; in 1960 it won six Championship rounds and again took the double title. The message could not have been clearer – go rear engined – and some had already done so by then.

The Coopers Charles and John, father and son, garage proprietors of Surbiton, Surrey, began in the raucous and primitive world of 500cc car racing, where the rear- (or mid-) engined layout was too logical to be ignored. '500s', later given International status as Formula 3, were launched as 'poor man's racers' in 1946, using motorcycle engines and transmissions. The Coopers, combining experience and enthusiasm, quickly confected one between two front suspension units sawn off scrap Fiat 'Topolino' baby cars. These

Clinching Cooper's title as World Champion Constructors in 1959, the young New Zealander Bruce McLaren won his first major race, the 1959 US Grand Prix, at Sebring in a works Cooper-Climax

were joined by side members of square tubing to produce an all-independently sprung four-wheeled chassis with minimum trouble. For power they used a JAP speedway racing engine, and with chain drive essential, where more logical than to fit the JAP just ahead of the rear wheels, driving them through a motorcycle gearbox? The final drive was mounted rigidly on the chassis, with double universally-jointed half-shafts, and the little cars worked so well that orders flowed in, and Coopers found themselves in the hurly-burly of manufacture.

Scrap Fiats quickly ran out so they began making their own suspension units, then their own light alloy wheels and other major parts, and soon Cooper cars were known wherever there was racing. After a dabble at front-mounted engines with the 1952–53 Formula 2 Cooper-Bristol which gave them an entrée into the Grand Prix world, they reverted to the old faith and developed, first 1100 and 1500cc sports cars renowned for their aerodynamic 'Manx tail' bodies,

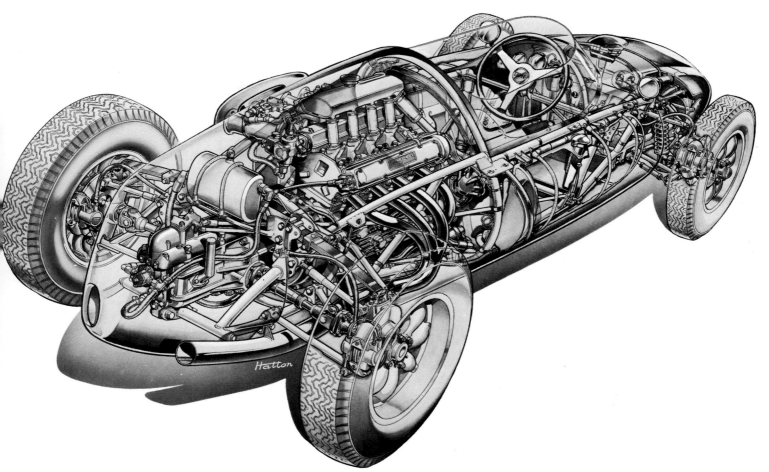

and then a rear-engined single-seater for the 1½-litre Formula 2 in 1956. The engine was a four-cylinder single-cam light alloy Coventry Climax, descendant of a fire pump unit; it drove through a four-speed gearbox behind the differential as on the pre-war Auto Union. The chassis was of welded tube, the suspension independent all round by transverse leaf springs, the bodywork light, simple and shapely, and the handling far more predictable and pleasant than the sinister oversteering rear-engined car of tradition. A 143 bhp five-bearing twin overhead camshaft engine, the Climax FPF, was the inevitable next step, and in 1957 F2 Coopers were lapping the tighter circuits at close on F1 lap speeds and not tiring their drivers half as much.

What followed was equally inevitable – 'dropping' a bigger engine into the 1000 lb car and trying Formula 1. Distinguished private entrant Rob Walker backed it, Coventry Climax stretched an FPF out to 1960 cc, Walker's mechanic Alf Francis fitted it, and Australian Jack Brabham drove it in the 1957 Monaco GP. He was up to third place with two laps to go when the fuel pump broke off, and he pushed home sixth. For 1958 the transverse leaf front spring gave way to coil springs, wishbones and an anti-

roll bar, and disc brakes and a new four-speed gearbox with ZF self-locking differential were fitted. Then Walker's car, adapted to run on the new compulsory Avgas, was sent to the Argentine GP in January 1958. Driver Stirling Moss first outraged the organisers with his 'English toy', and then he and Francis fooled the Ferrari and Maserati teams by 'rigging' an imminent pit stop, on to continue non-stop to win the race at record speed – on bald tyres!

When Moss took the Aintree 200 three months later, and Frenchman Trintignant won the next GP at Monaco, the seeds of the great racing revolution were well sewn. Not everyone liked it, but the coming of Coopers into the Grand Prix world meant more than rear-engine location; it brought the age of proprietary engines and other bought-out parts, while Rudge wire wheels gave way to light alloy 'bolt-ons' with wheel changes no longer featuring in the new, shorter Grands Prix. For 1959 Coventry Climax produced a full 2½-litre FPF to the dimensions 94 × 89·9 mm (2495 cc), giving 240 bhp at 6750 rpm in a 1060 lb car. A tendency to 'rear wheel steer' had been erased by fitting double wishbones to the rear suspension, and the season opened with encouraging wins at Goodwood and Silverstone. Then Brabham won the

The car that wrought a revolution in GP design, the 1959 Formula 1 Cooper-Climax which took Jack Brabham to his first World Championship. He won the Monaco and British GPs, Stirling Moss won the Portuguese and Italian GPs, and McLaren won the US GP. The Coventry Climax FPF engine drove through a four-speed gearbox behind the final drive; a multi-tubular frame, disc brakes and bolt-on alloy wheels contributed to a winning formula

Following the Indianapolis example, Grand Prix cars with proprietary engines and other components became fashionable with the advent of the Cooper in Formula 1. This is the 2½-litre Coventry Climax FPF unit which propelled them to so many successes. Designed by Walter Hassan and Harry Mundy, it was a light but sturdy twin-cam engine of straightforward concept, with excellent torque and a maximum output of 240 bhp at 6750 rpm in 1959

Monaco GP outright and followed up with the British GP at Aintree as well. Adding sundry high placings elsewhere, the Australian found himself 1959 World Champion, while Moss won the Portuguese and Italian GPs in a Walker car fitted with a special five-speed Colotti gearbox. Then Bruce McLaren of New Zealand added the United States GP to the Cooper Cars collection, and they deservedly won the 1959 Manufacturers' Championship.

While rival drawing boards groaned under plans for new rear-engined GP cars, the Coopers, designer Owen Maddock and Jack Brabham quietly prepared for their 1960 campaign. Brabham was the first of that talented breed, the driver/mechanic. He knew his car through and through, could diagnose and correct faults, and introduced the technique of on-the-spot adjustment of the suspension, wheel camber, etc. to secure the very best handling. Although it remained light, agile and simple, the 1960 Cooper was bigger and less fragile than earlier ones; it had a new multi-tubular frame, independent coil and wishbone suspension all round, a new five-speed gearbox and relocated fuel tanks. Yet it scaled only 1204 lb ready to race, and with the 2½-litre FPF Climax, this GP Cooper was good for over 180 mph.

World Champion Brabham became Champion again after winning the Dutch, Belgian, French, British and Portuguese Grands Prix in a sensational unbroken row, every one of them at record speed! Bruce McLaren contributed the Argentine GP, and Coopers justly became the Champion make for the second consecutive year. With this Mercedes-style display of total superiority, any lingering hints of 'Cooper luck' and 'flukey wins' were finally killed, and the most significant compliment of all to the modest Surbiton firm was the fact that in 1961 every serious car on the Grand Prix grids was rear engined.

Specification
Engine
Coventry Climax, four cylinders, in-line; bore and stroke 94 × 89·9 mm; capacity 2495 cc; twin overhead camshafts, two valves per cylinder; two Weber twin-choke carburetters; magneto ignition; maximum power, 240 bhp at 6750 rpm.
Transmission
Cooper five-speed gearbox in unit with final drive
Chassis
Multi-tubular frame; unequal length wishbones and coil springs at front and rear; Armstrong coaxial telescopic hydraulic dampers. Girling hydraulic disc brakes. Dunlop tyres.
Dimensions
Wheelbase, 7 ft 7 in; front track, 3 ft 10·5 in; rear track, 4 ft; dry weight, 1040 lb.

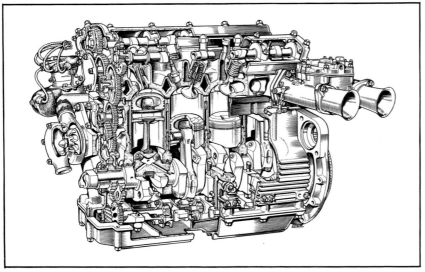

BRM 1½-litre V8

'After 14 years of struggling we have arrived at the summit.'

Raymond Mays

BRM of Bourne, Lincolnshire, have run almost equal with Ferrari in their long-term support of Grand Prix racing, going back to 1950, and even earlier on paper. If enthusiasm and optimism alone won races, British Racing Motors would have a victory list as long as Ferrari's, but alas, a good practical outlook, firm direction and adequate engineering and financial resources are other requisites. BRM had them all in their finest phase, the 1½-litre Formula from 1961 to 1965. After waiting 10 years for their first GP victory – Bonnier's Dutch win in 1959 – they waited another three years for the next, and when it came it unleashed what to victory-starved BRM seemed a flood of success – 11 GPs in four glorious seasons. The 1½-litre V8, with its characteristic deep, growling exhaust note, was the car that wrought this miracle.

In an era when proprietary engines were sapping the pedigree of British Formula 1 cars, this handsome BRM stood out as a complete one-make car with engine, transmission, chassis and bodywork all produced at Bourne. It was rear-engined, of course, BRM having taken the Cooper road in 1960, although the following year they, and other misguided British teams, were caught without a suitable engine through refusing to take the FIA's 1961–65 1½-litre Formula 1 seriously. Thus they had to resort to the 152bhp Formula 2 Coventry Climax FPF 4-cylinder unit, leaving Ferrari to win most of the races with his rear-engined Dino V6.

But while Bourne's cars played their customary role of also-rans during 1961, their designer Peter Berthon was hard at work on a new engine. Although he had to share blame for earlier BRM failures, equally Berthon merited great praise for his brilliant concept of their 1½-litre V8 high-speed engine. Its cylinders were angled at 90 degrees and measured 68·6 × 50·8mm, there were twin overhead camshafts to each bank beneath elegant finned covers, and the crankshaft ran in five Vandervell lead–indium thin-wall bearings. Important new features of the time were transistorised ignition (also used by Coventry Climax) and fuel injection, both manufactured by Lucas. Unlike magneto or coil ignition, the new electronic system could provide sparks at the rate of 1000 per second if required, an important consideration since in 1962 the BRM delivered 188bhp, with a peak of 193 at

Patience rewarded: 12 years passed before the much-vaunted BRM Grand Prix venture bore full fruit, but Graham Hill's four 1962 victories and resultant World Championship were all the sweeter for the long wait. Here the Londoner is about to take the Karussel banked turn at Nürburgring, where he won the German GP with the Berthon-designed 1½-litre V8 car

Although Graham Hill
made the Monaco GP
particularly his own with
five victories, the 1962 race
proved unlucky for him;
driving the early V8 BRM
with 'stackpipe' exhausts he
was leading with seven
laps to go when the oil
pressure and his chances
vanished

10250rpm, and during its lifetime attained a prodigious 12000rpm.

Fuel injection was into the ports on the inside of the vee, each injector having its own air intake trumpet. The new F1 rulings stipulated 100 octane fuel only, so several extra bhp over carburetters and quicker throttle response were particularly valuable; the fuel, 31·5 gallons in all, was carried in aircraft-type rubber tanks each side of the driver's seat. A multi-tube space-frame was used, carrying all-round independent suspension by wishbones and coil spring/ damper units; the magnesium wheels and disc brakes were both by Dunlop, and the exhausts discharged upwards through short pipes with megaphones, although these tended to break off and were changed for normal tailpipes in mid-season. The FIA's minimum weight limit was 450kg (990lb) but the BRM was 84lb over this; it was, indeed, a good, solid car, driven by a good, solid man, Graham Hill who, with the new team manager-cum-chief engineer Tony Rudd, turned BRM's fortunes at a time when their owner, Sir Alfred Owen, appalled at spending over £1 million for one victory, had demanded two major wins that year at pain of closing down. Instead of two he got four, and both the World Manufacturers' and Drivers' Championships as well!

Hill began early by winning the 100-mile Glover Trophy race at the Easter Goodwood, then gave BRM another tonic by beating Clark's Lotus on the very finish line in the Silverstone International Trophy. Next he won the Dutch GP, led at Monaco until his engine gave out seven laps from the end, was second in the Belgian GP, then won the German and Italian GPs, bringing to reality Raymond Mays' 17-year-old dream of seeing a BRM win these continental classics. And in the final 1962 GP in South Africa Hill ran second to Clark's Lotus until the latter's engine failed him, then won the race and with it the World Championship.

For 1963 the BRM V8 became a 200bhp monocoque, but could only beat the lighter Lotus on reliability; the determined Hill won the Monaco and US GPs, and repeated both these victories in 1964 and 1965. In the latter year, aided by Harry Weslake, output rose to 212bhp at no less than 11500rpm, and Scotsman Jackie Stewart joined Hill in the team, winning the International Trophy at Silverstone and the Italian GP.

The new 3 litre Formula began in 1966, but the valiant BRM V8, enlarged to 2 litres, served on. Stewart and Hill went out to the Antipodes for the Tasman Cup series, the Scot taking four races and the Championship, while the Londoner won the New Zealand and Australian GPs. Stewart then won the 1966 Monaco GP on 2 litres and finally, squeezing the last from the juiciest of Bourne oranges, he repeated Graham Hill's Tasman double by winning both the New Zealand and Australian GPs in 1967 – by which time Bourne were back in the doldrums with their latest cars....

Specification
Engine
90degree V8; bore and stroke, 68·5 × 50·8mm; capacity 1498cc; four overhead camshafts operating two valves per cylinder; Lucas port-type fuel injection; Lucas transistorised ignition; maximum power, 188bhp at 10250rpm in 1962, rising to 212bhp at 11500rpm by 1965.

Transmission
BRM five-speed gearbox in unit with final drive.
Chassis
Tubular space frame in 1962; monocoque, 1963–65. Double wishbone and coil spring/damper unit suspension at front and rear. Armstrong coaxial dampers. Dunlop hydraulic disc brakes. Dunlop tyres.
Dimensions
Wheelbase, 7ft 5·8in; front track, 4ft 4·5in; rear track, 4ft 4·25in; dry weight, 1090lb.

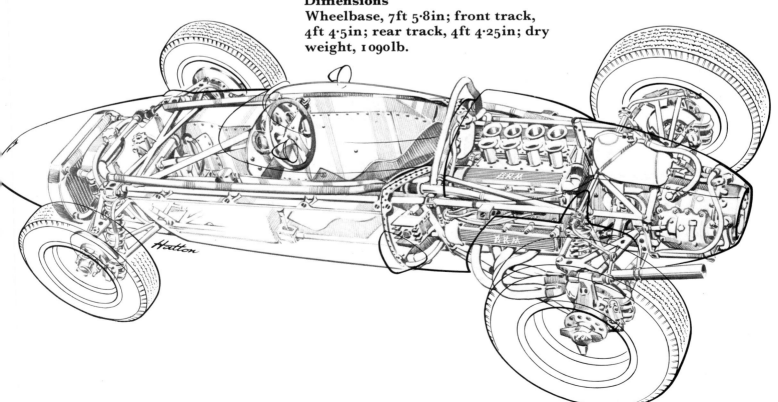

Flat-8 Porsche 804

'In September 1961 four Porsche mechanics swore an oath not to shave any more until a Porsche won a GP race. After Rouen their fine beards are off . . .'

'Christophorus'

Although it bore his honoured name and carried on the rear-engined tradition of his pre-war Auto Unions, the 1962 Formula 1 Porsche came 10 years after the death of the eminent Austrian designer, Dr Ferdinand Porsche. The Porsche marque, founded by the Doktor and his son Ferry in 1947, inherited strong racing interests which they have pursued ever since, and the flat-eight F1 car was a fascinating departure from their policy in the 1960s of fielding production-based competition machinery. It also contributed refreshing technical variety to the initially derided 1½-litre GP Formula of 1961–65 which brought V8s, narrow and wide angle V6s, flat eights and, finally, V12s in competition with each other.

Porsche began single-seater racing in 1959 with Formula 2 flat-fours based on the RSK sports-racing car, Bonnier winning the Ger-

man and Modena GPs of 1960 with one, while Moss, in a car loaned to Rob Walker, was first at Aintree and at Zeltweg in Austria. These successes encouraged the Stuttgart-Zuffenhausen establishment to run the same cars in 1961 under the new Formula 1, while working on an all-new flat-eight design, the Type 804, which appeared the following year after a prolonged gestation.

Like every Porsche, it was air-cooled, having a horizontal plastic fan driven off the timing gear, with the engine fully shrouded. The eight cylinders, in two horizontally opposed banks of four, were individually machined in aluminium, and their bores treated with a sprayed coating of molybdenum steel called Ferral. Bore and stroke were $66 \times 54{\cdot}6$ mm (1494 cc), and the separate aluminium heads had inserted valve seats and supported a one-piece aluminium casting containing the twin overhead camshafts of each bank, driven by shafts and bevels

Bringing welcome variety to the Grand Prix scene, Porsche's 1962 Formula 1 car had a 184bhp 1½-litre horizontally-opposed eight-cylinder engine with aircooling, a six-speed gearbox and torsion bar suspension all round

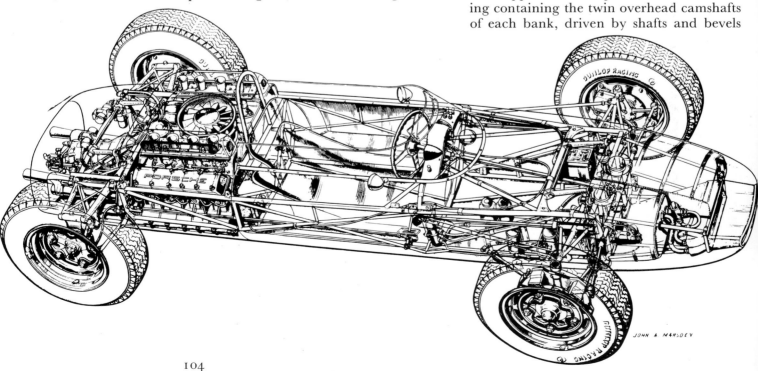

from the crankshaft. This was a one-piece unit running in nine plain bearings with split connecting rods; there were four double-choke Weber carburetters, with intakes in twin gauzed housings projecting above the engine cover, while a battery, four coils and two distributors sustained two plugs per cylinder.

Output of this interesting engine was 180bhp at 9000rpm, rising to 184bhp at 9300rpm by end of season. The 804 had a rather heavy frame of triangulated tubular space-type, with all-round independent suspension by wishbones, torsion bars and Koni coaxial hydraulic dampers mounted inside the bodywork. Porsche made virtually *all* their car, including the disc brakes and rather homely-looking bolt-on alloy wheels, and the Type 804 was very low but rather wide by 1962 standards, its frontal area increased by a partially reclining seat from which the large Dan Gurney sprouted well above the windshield.

Two cars made their debut at Zandvoort in the Dutch GP, there to encounter the expected teething troubles, although one survived to place seventh. Ill luck struck when Bonnier crashed one car while testing in Germany, and the other was put out of the Monaco GP after an opening lap *imbroglio* for which driver Gurney was blameless. The team withdrew from the Belgian GP for rebuilding and revision in several aspects. The front suspension was braced with trailing radius arms, an anti-roll bar was fitted at the rear, and the Koni dampers were replaced by Bilstein inert gas type. The disc brakes and gearchange were both improved, and the seat altered to lower the driver, necessitating a detachable steering wheel.

Both cars then went to Rouen for the French GP, where Gurney emerged from a race of attrition to score a popular victory. A week later the silver cars took a one-two finish in their 'local' race, the Solitude GP outside Stuttgart. The American Dan Gurney then finished third in the German GP while the Swede Joakim Bonnier won the Swiss Mountain Championship hillclimb at Ollons-Villars at record speed. Stuttgart tried hard by weight-saving and stream-lining wiles to keep up with the opposition in the Italian GP; they lost 25lb by urgent paring, faired the suspension wishbones and fitted flush wheel discs. Gurney was disputing third position when his transmission failed, and a final effort in the United States GP brought him a disappointing fifth, again after holding third place.

Finding their FI programme unduly ex-

pensive, and faced with further expense in producing a monocoque chassis and switching to fuel injection if they were to offer worthy opposition, Ferry Porsche and his fellow directors took the sad but sensible decision to withdraw from Grand Prix racing. But their development work on the flat eight was not wasted; they produced a 2-litre version for sports car racing and hill-climbing, and later applied the acquired 'know-how' to the fantastically successful flat-12 5·4-litre turbocharged 1000bhp CanAm cars of the 1970s.

Dan Gurney of California, winner with the flat-eight Porsche of the French GP at Rouen and the Solitude GP, also took a close third place in the 1962 German GP; he is seen here on Nürburgring's famous Karussel during practice for that race

Specification
Engine
180 degrees, eight cylinders, aircooled; bore and stroke, 66 × 54·6mm; capacity, 1494cc; four overhead camshafts operating two valves per cylinder; four double-choke Weber carburetters; battery, coil and distributor ignition; max power, 180bhp at 9000rpm, rising to 184bhp at 9300rpm.
Transmission
Porsche six-speed all-synchromesh gearbox in unit with final drive.
Chassis
Multi-tubular space frame; double wishbone and longitudinal torsion bar independent suspension front and rear. Koni hydraulic telescopic or Bilstein inert gas-filled dampers. Porsche hydraulic disc brakes. Dunlop tyres.
Dimensions
Wheelbase, 7ft 6·5in; front track, 4ft 3·25in; rear track, 4ft 2·75in; dry weight, 1023lb.

Lotus 25 'Monocoque'

'The tube is the stiffest form of structure known. Moreover, it gives you more space.'

Colin Chapman

For six years racing cars had armoured wood frames; for over thirty they used channel steel; for nearly twenty years after that they built on two large-diameter steel tubes, and for eight years the multi-tube space-frame ruled. Suddenly, in May 1962, all separate chassis of any kind were rendered obsolete when that brilliant engineering adventurer Colin Chapman FRSA, B.Sc. introduced his Lotus 25 monocoque at Zandvoort for the Dutch GP. 'Monocoque' literally means 'single shell', but the need for an open top

half made the Lotus structure more a semi-monocoque or, in racing parlance, a 'bath-tub'. Such nuances apart, the principle brought Chapman's Lotus concern double World Championships for drivers and manu-facturers in three years, and set the entire racing world copying him.

The idea was nurtured by the challenge of the 1½-litre Formula 1 with its 998lb mini-mum weight limit. Obliged to use the same Coventry Climax engines as other British makers, Chapman aimed to outwit them by building smaller, lighter, cleaner cars with better roadholding. He began with the space-framed Lotus 21 on which, to reduce drag, the front coil spring/damper suspen-sion units were neatly tucked away inside the slender nose and worked by the boxed canti-lever top wishbones. At the rear the Chap-man ingenuity produced leech-like wheel adhesion by using a single-link top suspen-sion member, reversed lower wishbones and twin radius arms each side, while rubber

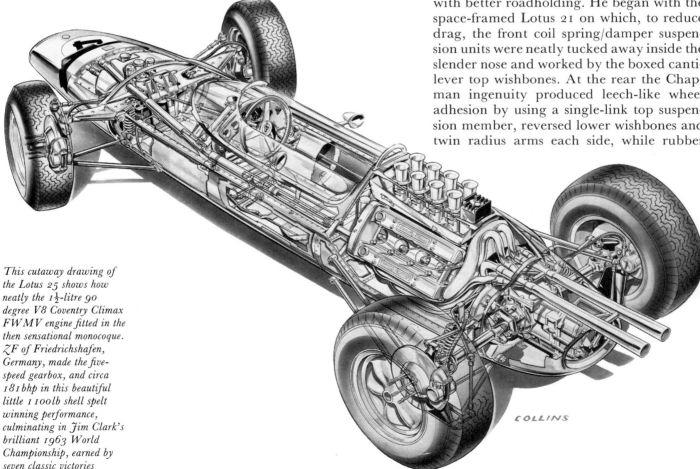

This cutaway drawing of the Lotus 25 shows how neatly the 1½-litre 90 degree V8 Coventry Climax FWMV engine fitted in the then sensational monocoque. ZF of Friedrichshafen, Germany, made the five-speed gearbox, and circa 181bhp in this beautiful little 1100lb shell spelt winning performance, culminating in Jim Clark's brilliant 1963 World Championship, earned by seven classic victories

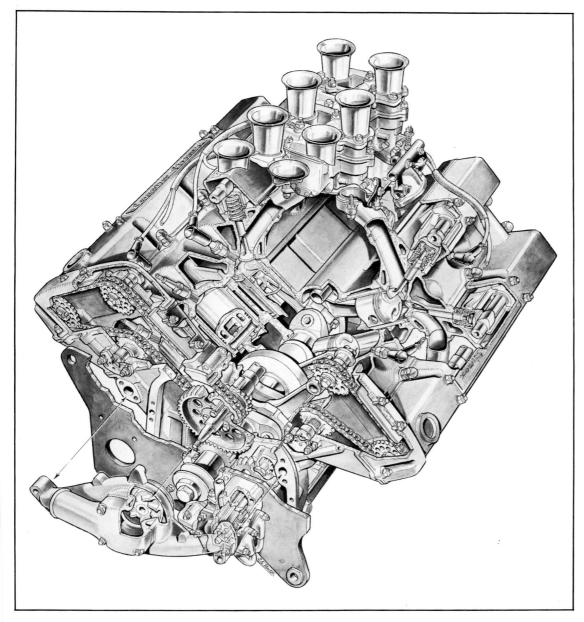

'doughnuts' in the final drive dispensed with splined half-shafts.

This exquisite little car agitated the Ferraris throughout 1961 and brought Lotus their first *grande epreuve* when Innes Ireland won the US GP. He also won the Solitude and Zeltweg GPs, while Jim Clark took three races in South Africa, by which time Coventry Climax had delivered their first FWMV V8 engine to replace the four-cylinder FPF. On twin double-choke Weber carburetters this meant 181 bhp instead of 153, and with some small suspension modifications, a slightly (1 in) longer wheelbase, a humped engine cover and two megaphoned exhausts aimed rearward like Browning guns in a Lancaster turret, the Lotus 21 became the 24. Driven by Clark this won two non-Championship British races early in 1962 and looked all set for a good season when it, and every other F1

car, was outdated by the sensational 25 monocoque at Zandvoort.

Although there was the D-type Jaguar of 1954 and an experimental 1955 BRM as earlier examples of stressed skin construction, it was while working on a prototype Lotus Elan sports car with backbone frame that Chapman visualised a frameless single-seater formed from a widened backbone able to accommodate the driver. Built from Alclad aluminium and steel sheet painstakingly riveted up on a jig, the structure comprised two hollow rectangular side members or pontoons, joined by a floor pan, dash panel, front engine bulkhead and suspension mountings. The driver's seat between the pontoons was steeply inclined to reduce frontal area, while filling the space behind and below it was a triangular rubber bag fuel tank, with two others in the pontoons, which formed a

little Lotus 25 went out with clutch trouble; the transmission played up again at Monaco, but third time out at Spa, the car found its form and Jim Clark won the Belgian GP at 131·9mph – an outstanding speed for a 1½-litre car. He went on to win four more F1 races, including the British and US GPs, which put him in contention with Graham Hill of BRM for the World Championship title. In the final round, the South African GP, Clark needed to win outright; he led until three-quarters-distance, when a small bolt came out of the engine and released the lifeblood of his Climax engine.

If the monocoque lost the 1962 Championship, there was no doubt about its 1963 victory. The cars now had Lucas fuel injection and about 195bhp, and Jim Clark, that matchless Scot, won the Belgian, Dutch, French, British, Italian, Mexican and South African GPs and simply ran away with the title, while Lotus became the Champion Manufacturers. In 1964 three more GPs fell to Clark, after which the gallant 25 was superseded by the 33 with 32-valve Coventry Climax engine. With this Clark took his second Championship, and Lotus theirs, after six epic victories in 1965. By then every Formula 1 marque bar two had changed over to monocoque construction, in deference to the genius of Colin Chapman.

Specification

Engine
Coventry Climax 90degree V8; bore and stroke, 63×60mm; capacity 1498cc; four overhead camshafts, two valves per cylinder; twin double-choke Weber carburetters in 1962; Lucas fuel injection in 1963–64; Lucas electronic ignition; maximum power, 181bhp at 8200rpm in 1962, rising to about 195bhp in 1963.
Transmission
Five-speed ZF gearbox (synchromesh on four upper ratios) in unit with final drive.
Chassis
Monocoque construction.
Front suspension by wishbones and inboard coil spring/damper units; rear suspension with single upper transverse links, reversed lower wishbones and coil spring/damper units. Girling hydraulic disc brakes. Dunlop tyres.
Dimensions
Wheelbase, 7ft 7in; front track, 4ft 4in; rear track, 4ft 5·2in; dry weight, 1100lb.

'If it looks right . . .' The great Jim Clark in Colin Chapman's highly efficient 1½-litre GP cars. Top to bottom: at Rouen in 1962, in the slightly modified 1963 25, and in the improved 33 with the more powerful 32-valve Climax engine in 1965

fork at the rear wherein the Climax V8 engine contributed to structural stiffness.

The monocoque hull was 12lb lighter than the old space-frame, while the elimination of the aluminium tanks and fittings saved nearly 50lb more. It was more expensive to produce, but torsional rigidity was much higher, which meant improved roadholding and handling, greater security for the driver and negligible maintenance with no flexing or cracking, as in tubular space frames. The Lotus 24 front and rear suspensions were built in, and the same ZF five-speed gearbox employed. After holding a brief lead in the Dutch GP the fascinating

1½-litre
V12 Honda

'They're really after a chunk of the world automobile market . . . It'll take a few years, but they'll get their share all right!'

Ronnie Bucknum

On proud display in the reception hall of the Honda Motor Co's big main plain in Chuo-Ku, Tokyo, is a small, off-white racing car with black-enamelled suspension, the 'rising sun' painted atop the bonnet, and a notice in Japanese recording the part it played in the International hurly-burly that is modern motor racing. It won just one Grand Prix, the very last of the 1961–65 1½-litre Formula 1, but it was a highly convincing victory, achieved only 14 months after the cars from the Far East entered an intensely competitive field entirely new to them. Honda are, of course, giants in the motorcycle world, extremely well versed in the extraction of the last iota of power from tiny multi-cylinder engines in international motorcycle racing. They launched their first car, the neat S600 two-seater sports, in 1962, after which their principal, Soichiro Honda, decided to enter Grand Prix racing to help spread the name of Honda more widely.

The most interesting part of the first Honda F1 car, type-numbered the RA271, was undoubtedly its engine. Seeking the highest possible output from 1½ litres, technical director Sekiguchi, engine specialist Irimagiri and development engineer Nakamura opted for 12 small cylinders at 60 degrees, with four tiny valves to each one worked by twin overhead camshafts on each bank, and a prodigious crankshaft speed able to exceed 13000rpm. Then, like the great Gioacchino Colombo in his last racing design, the abortive under-financed Bugatti Type 256 of 1956, they set the engine transversely at the rear instead of lengthwise.

As on Honda racing motorcycles (and the Bugatti), the camshaft drive and power take-off were central, driving through a six-speed gearbox between the engine and the final drive. Bore and stroke were 58·1 × 47mm (1495cc), and the output in 1964 was an impressive 220bhp at 11000rpm. The motor-cycle inheritance was further evident in the needle roller bearings for crankshaft and big ends, and the initial use of six twin-choke Keihin motorcycle carburetters. A chassis with central monocoque section carried the engine, final drive and rear suspension in a tubular sub-frame; suspension was by in-board coil spring/damper units at front and rear, and Dunlop disc brakes were employed. Unusual at a time of Dunlop monopoly was

New colours: off white with a red 'rising sun' symbol was the uniform adopted by Honda of Japan when they entered Formula 1 GP racing. Richie Ginther takes his RA272 into the Gasworks hairpin while practising for the 1965 Monaco GP

the use of Goodyear tyres, the American company first entering Grand Prix racing in 1964 with both Brabham and Honda.

After extensive development work at the Zandvoort circuit in Holland, Honda and their driver, Ronnie Bucknum from California, went in at the deep end by choosing the German GP at the difficult Nürburgring for their race debut. Troubles with overheating and erratic braking dogged them, but Bucknum had climbed from 22nd to 11th place when his steering failed and he left the road four laps from the end, though still classified 13th. The Japanese one-car team then switched from carburetters to indirect fuel injection for the Italian GP at Monza, where improved pick-up helped Bucknum up to fifth place before more braking and overheating problems forced him out. Retirement in the US GP with the same maladies was a dispiriting end to their season, but for 1965 the very experienced Ferrari

On test in its native land — the little 12-cylinder 1500cc Honda at the Suzuka circuit; despite its thin exhaust pipes it produced impressively busy noises

Showing the transverse location of the 60 degree

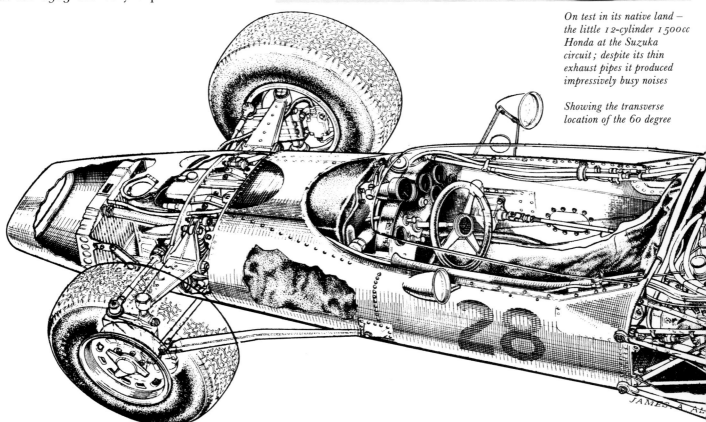

and BRM driver Richie Ginther joined the team and three new RA272 cars were built.

A broken final drive ended Ginther's first race at Monaco on the first lap, after which the Japanese universal joints were replaced by Australian Repco units supplied by Jack Brabham. At Spa the Honda's 230bhp on fuel injection had its effect, Ginther getting a second row start, briefly holding fourth place and finishing sixth. Both cars vacated

the French GP with ignition trouble, but in the British GP Ginther was third fastest in practice, led the entire field off the mark, dropped to third place, then had to retire with fuel injection defects. In the Dutch GP Ginther shared second place on the grid with Jim Clark and led the race for two laps until the little V12's beefy top end torque caught him out and he spun twice, eventually scoring another sixth place. The team then

12-cylinder engine and six-speed gearbox ahead of the final drive, the truncated monocoque chassis and the top rocker arms to the inboard front suspension. Given more development and time, the claimed engine output of between 220 and 230bhp at over 11000rpm should have brought more success

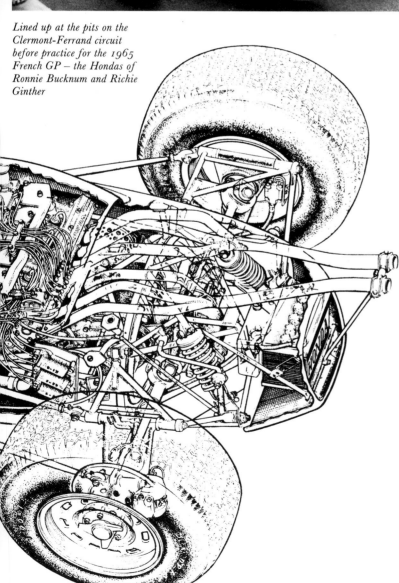

Lined up at the pits on the Clermont-Ferrand circuit before practice for the 1965 French GP – the Hondas of Ronnie Bucknum and Richie Ginther

gave the German GP a miss for some important improvements, the engines having new crankcases and lowered mountings, while the rear suspension was modified and the bodywork slimmed.

At Monza for the Italian GP it was Bucknum who did best for Honda in practice with sixth fastest time, although engine troubles eliminated both cars from the race. More work for Nakamura and his men followed with a new rear subframe to be fitted to one car, giving a 2·5in longer wheelbase for the US GP at Watkins Glen, where Ginther made second fastest practice time. A first lap spin unfortunately set him back, and eventually he placed seventh, while Bucknum was 11th, signifying Honda's first full team finish. Then came the final 1965 race, the Mexican GP on the 3·2-mile Magdalena-Mixhuca circuit, 1·5 miles above sea level. That the Honda fuel injection system worked well in such conditions showed in practice, with Ginther in row 2 and Bucknum in row 4, and in the race Ginther took an immediate lead from the Lotus, Brabham, Ferrari and BRM opposition and stayed firmly ahead throughout the race, to win at a record 94·26mph. It was both his and Honda's first Grand Prix win, and with Bucknum finishing fifth it was a satisfying if unwelcome end to the 1½-litre Formula for the Oriental cars, just when they had found their proper form.

Specification
Engine
60 degree V12; bore and stroke, 58·1 × 47mm; capacity, 1495cc; four overhead camshafts operating four valves per cylinder; six Keihin twin-choke carburetters in 1964, indirect fuel injection in 1965; coil and battery ignition; maximum power, 220bhp at 11000rpm in 1964, rising to 230bhp at 12000rpm in 1965.
Transmission
Six-speed gearbox in unit with final drive.
Chassis
Monocoque centre-section with engine/suspension sub-frame. Suspension by wishbone and coil spring/Koni damper units front and rear.
Dunlop disc brakes. Goodyear tyres.
Dimensions
Wheelbase, 7ft 6·1in; front track, 4ft 5·1in; rear track, 5ft 9in; dry weight, 1155lb in 1964, 1096lb in 1965.
Variants
Inboard rear brakes also tried.

Indianapolis Lotus-Ford

'Indy's hallowed bricks will never be the same.'

Gordon H. Jennings, 'Road & Track,' 1963

Although undoubtedly the leading British racing car designer during the past 15 years, even Colin Chapman had to follow in someone else's footsteps sometimes. He joined the rush to go rear-engined in 1960 after Cooper had pointed the way, and two years after the Surbiton firm and Jack Brabham had put a European foot in the Indianapolis door, he too built a car for America's highly lucrative 500 Miles race. But whereas Coopers in 1961 had to make do with a basically Formula 1 Coventry Climax engine enlarged to 2·7 litres, Chapman in 1963 shrewdly secured the support of the US Ford Motor Company in providing special 4·2-litre V8 engines to fit into two Lotus cars. The resultant combination totally disrupted the Indianapolis 'establishment' and rendered the big, lumpish front-engined 'Indy roadsters' obsolete overnight.

Chapman's interest was kindled by the American driver Dan Gurney, who at his own expense, took the Lotus chief out to Indianapolis in 1962 and helped in negotiating with Ford. The engine which they supplied was a 4·2-litre version of their Fairlane pushrod overhead valve 90 degree V8 series-production unit, giving 375 bhp at

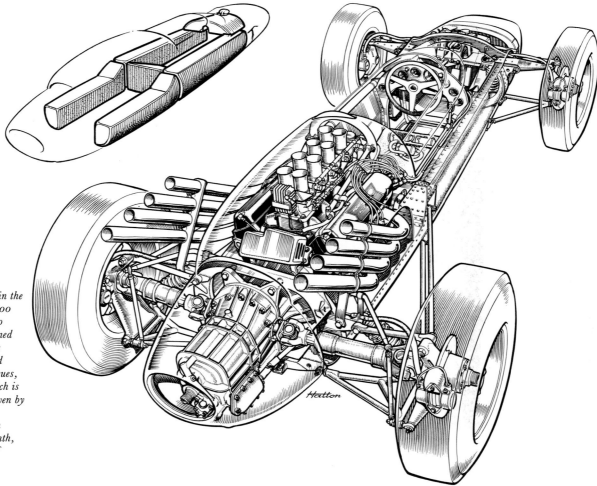

Chapman's first effort in the famous Indianapolis 500 came in 1963 with two pushrod Ford V8-engined Lotus 29s. These were virtually reinforced and lengthened 25 monocoques, the construction of which is shown separately. Driven by Jim Clark and Dan Gurney, they finished a strong second and seventh, giving fair warning of things to come

7200rpm on four Weber twin-choke carburetters. It was installed in a modified Lotus 25 F1 monocoque, lengthened to give a 5in longer wheelbase to meet USAC requirements, and to accommodate the Ford engine (and Californian Dan Gurney's long legs in one car); the track was over 3in wider. The car, called the Lotus 29, had six fuel tanks carrying 50 gallons overall, and a dry weight of 1131lb to the average 'roadster's' 1680lb. To counter all-left hand turn centrifugal effects at the 2·5-mile oblong, offset suspension located the hull asymetrically, to some detriment of appearance but not performance. Jim Clark's 'little green bug', running on gasoline, staggered everyone by finishing a strong second to Parnelli Jones's Watson-built 'roadster', powered by a nitro-methane-burning Offenhauser engine. The British Lotus only lost the lead through poor pitwork, while Dan Gurney finished seventh after making an extra stop.

After this demonstration by a 'rookie' driver in a 'rookie' car, Clark went on to win the Milwaukee 200 Mile USAC race, with Gurney third to make it a Lotus sandwich around A.J.Foyt's 'roadster'. The latter retaliated at Trenton, where the two 29s set the pace but blew up.

The upstart British team returned to Indianapolis in 1964 with improved cars designated Type 34, these having increased suspension offset and transmission alterations, and Ford engines much revised with new twin overhead camshaft heads, four valves per cylinder, Hilborn petrol injection, and about 410bhp at 8000rpm. Clark qualified at a shattering 158·828mph, over 7·5mph above the previous record, but it availed him little, for although he and Gurney had the fastest cars on the track, trouble with 'chunking' Dunlop tyres put them both out of the race, which marked the last victory by a traditional 'roadster'. Later that season both the Milwaukee and Trenton 200 Mile races fell to a Lotus 34, driven by the former 'roadster' pilot Parnelli Jones, now thoroughly converted to 'the funny little Limey cars'.

In 1965 Lotus were back for their third try at the great American classic. The four-cam Ford motor was now adapted to run on alcohol, its output rising to 500bhp, and three new cars, type-numbered the Lotus 38, were built with Len Terry as chief designer. A full monocoque hull was adopted rather than the earlier 'bathtub' structure, remarkably slim lines being achieved despite the need to carry 58 gallons of fuel. Suspension, as before, comprised Armstrong coil spring/damper units mounted inboard at the front and outboard at the rear, with off-setting to help cope with 'Indy' conditions. Two 38s ran as Ford-backed factory entries for Clark and Bobby Johns, while the third went to Dan Gurney, and this time there were no mistakes. Jim Clark led all but 10 of the 200 laps to win the 1965 '500' at a record 150·68mph, taking a total of $166621 (over £75000) in prize money.

This was the first European win at Indianapolis for 49 years, the first ever for a rear-engined car, and the first for a British car. Scotland's greatest driver headed a 1964 Type 34 Lotus-Ford by over five miles, while a 29 was fifth and the second works 38, seventh in heady vindication of Colin Chapman's brilliance. To complete the revolution, 'Indy'-type Lotus-Fords again won the USAC races at Trenton and Milwaukee, thoroughly implanting modern rear-engine mindedness where the famous but grotesque and outdated 'roadsters' had reigned for far too long. Clark scored his second Indianapolis second placing with the same four-cam Ford-engined Lotus 38 in the 1966 race, in which all but one of the cars competing were rear-engined. In 1961 all but one were front-engined, so that in five years John Cooper's point, forcefully driven home by Colin Chapman, was well and truly taken by the US establishment.

Great day: Jim Clark grins happily after his superb 1965 500 Mile race victory in the Lotus 38 powered by a four-cam Ford V8 engine giving 500bhp on alcohol. Other Lotuses finished second, fifth and seventh, and as this marked the first European win at Indianapolis in 49 years, it was a real joy day for Colin Chapman and his team

Specification
Engine
Ford USA 90 degree V8; bore and stroke, 96·5 × 72·8mm; capacity, 4261cc; four overhead camshafts, operating four valves per cylinder; Hilborn-Travers fuel injection; electronic ignition; maximum power, 500bhp at 8000 rpm.
Transmission
ZF two-speed gearbox in unit with final drive.
Chassis
Monocoque construction. Front suspension by wishbones and inboard Armstrong coil spring/damper units; rear suspension by single top link, reversed bottom A-bracket, twin radius arms and exposed Armstrong coil spring/damper units. Girling disc brakes in 15 in Halibrand cast magnesium wheels. Firestone tyres.
Dimensions
Wheelbase, 8ft; track, 5ft front and rear; dry weight, 1250lb.
Maximum speed
200mph plus.

3-litre Repco-Brabham

'Nobody could tie that kangaroo down . . .'

Philip Turner, 'Motor'

Many owners of V8 Rovers may well be surprised to learn that the smooth power of their car has a close if coincidental kinship with a highly successful Grand Prix car. The engines in both came from a common root, General Motors of Detroit, who developed an advanced 3½-litre linerless light alloy 90 degree V8 with pushrod overhead valves for a new Oldsmobile 'compact' model, but then dropped it owing to quantity production problems. Whereas Rover acquired the overhead valve design outright and improved it, the Repco Engineering group of Melbourne, Australia, endowed the alloy block with new single overhead camshaft heads, a new Laystall crankshaft, Daimler connecting rods and other special parts, and produced a racing engine.

The Australian designer Phil Irving and Repco chief engineer Frank Hallam were responsible for this clever adaptation, their first objective being the 2½-litre Tasman Formula, with a larger sports car unit next on the list. Then Jack Brabham, World Champion in 1959 and 1960 with Coopers, and driver/manufacturer of his own cars since 1961, came on the scene. 1966 was the first year of the new 3-litre Formula 1, and

with Coventry Climax withdrawing and a new H16 BRM unit threatening development problems, Brabham sought alternative power. Being an Australian, he had particular influence with Repco, who had supported his racing since 1964 and had wide experience of building up special 2·5 Climax 'Tasman' engines, using their own bearings, pistons, liners, valves, etc. as well as the Oldsmobile conversions, and were thus admirably equipped to tackle a 3-litre adaptation of the American unit.

The original bore of 88·9mm was retained, this with a stroke of 60·3mm giving 2996cc. Dispensing with the single central camshaft and designing separate single-cam heads with chain timing gear drive posed tricky problems, but the result was a simple, straightforward engine unavoidably retaining parallel in-line valves, yet possessing excellent torque at low and medium crankshaft speeds, albeit with an initial output of under 300bhp at 7800rpm when Ferrari were claiming 360bhp for their 3-litre V12. With delays in other new engines, several British contenders had to use enlarged 1½-litre F1 units, whereas the new 3-litre Repco-Brabham BT19 appeared bright and

Winning at Brands: Jack Brabham in the 1966 British GP, his Repco-Brabham displaying its writhing snakepit of exhaust pipes

Denny Hulme, second home in the 1966 British GP at Brands Hatch, wrestles with the BT20 at Druids corner

early on January 1st, 1966, for the South African GP, first race to the new Formula.

On paper its championship chances looked meagre, with that single-cam engine and a space-frame in the 'monocoque' age. But 'old fox' Brabham and his designer Ron Tauranac reasoned that such a frame was more easily built and repaired by a small works than the costlier monocoque, while they also stuck to the exposed front coil springs they knew, rather than tuck them tidily away out of the airstream, as others did. The BT19 was, in fact, an adaptation of a 1965 F1 type prepared to take the abortive flat-16 1½-litre Coventry Climax engine that was never raced, and its design conservatism was offset by a pleasingly low dry weight of 1142lb (the Formula stipulated a minimum of 500kg or 1100lb), good roadholding and, they hoped, by engine reliability.

This was not immediately realised, for Brabham had to retire from the South African GP with fuel injection trouble after leading and making fastest lap. It took another retirement at Syracuse before the car was *au point*, when the Repco's excellent torque paid off at Silverstone and Brabham defeated Surtees' factory Ferrari to take the BRDC International Trophy plus a new lap record. Gearbox trouble intervened at Monaco, at Spa he was fourth, and then came a typical run of Brabham wins – four classics on the trot in the French, British, Dutch and German GPs, which with a second place in the Mexican GP earned the talented Australian his third World Championship and the first by a driver/manufacturer, while the marque Repco-Brabham won the Manufacturers' title.

During 1966 an improved car, the BT20, had been built with a modified space-frame, a 1·5in longer wheelbase and an inch more track, slightly wider body, 15in wheels rather than 13in and other detail improvements It was raced by New Zealander

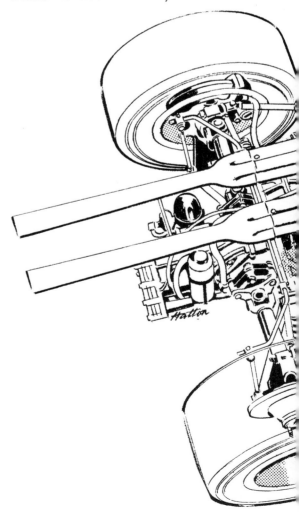

Denny Hulme, who took several good placings with it that season, and then won the Monaco GP in 1967. Meantime, Ron Tauranac had produced a third car, the BT24, based on the smaller Formula 2 Brabham but with its wheelbase extended by 1·75in, a Hewland F2-type five-speed gearbox, and a much modified Repco engine. This had new blocks, with the exhaust pipes disposed much more neatly inside the vee instead of the unruly pipes snaking around the suspension radius arms on the earlier cars.

Several extra bhp were even more welcome, although many rivals were surprised when the BT24s won three Grands Prix in 1967, Brabham taking the French and Canadian events, and Hulme the German. With his Monaco win in the BT20, plus cumulative points from other good placings including three seconds and three thirds, Hulme emerged as World Champion, with Jack Brabham as runner-up. The latter had compensation in non-Championship wins in the Spring Cup and Gold Cup races at Oulton Park, and in Repco-Brabham's second consecutive triumph in the Manufacturers' Championship – a magnificent achievement by one of the greatest driver/manufacturers ever, in cars that were simpler and cheaper than any of their opponents.

Specification
Engine
Repco 90 degree V8; bore and stroke, 88·9 × 60·3mm; capacity, 2996cc; single overhead camshafts operating two valves per cylinder; Lucas port fuel injection; coil and distributor ignition (BT19), then Lucas Opus transistorised ignition; maximum power, 285 bhp at 7800rpm (BT19), rising to ca. 310bhp at 7800rpm (BT24).
Transmission
Hewland five-speed gearbox in unit with ZF limited-slip differential.
Chassis
Multi-tubular space frame. Front suspension by double wishbones and

Clean and simple: a cutaway drawing of the Tauranac-designed Formula 1 Repco-Brabham, shown in 1967 form with the exhaust ports of the single-cam V8 engine inside the cylinder banks. The tubular chassis and outboard-sprung front suspension ignored Formula 1 fashion but proved their worth in dependability; this Anglo-Australian car took Jack Brabham to his third World Championship in 1966, and Denny Hulme to his first in 1967

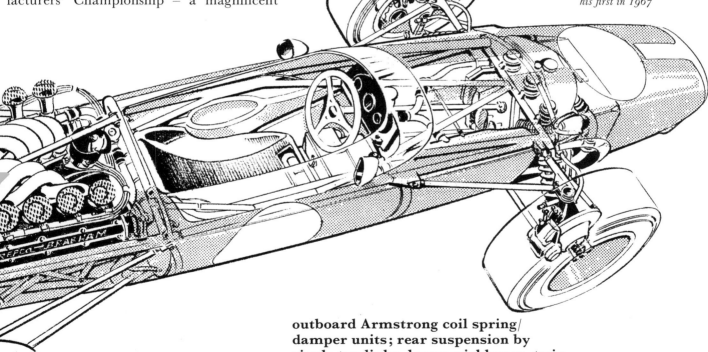

outboard Armstrong coil spring/damper units; rear suspension by single top links, lower wishbones, twin radius arms and Armstrong coil spring/damper units. Girling disc brakes. Goodyear tyres.
Dimensions
Wheelbase, 7ft 8in (BT19), 7ft 9·5in (BT20), 7ft 10in (BT24); front track, 4ft 5·5in (BT19), 4ft 6·5in (BT20), 4ft 4·5in (BT24); dry weight (approx.), 1142lb (BT19), 1210lb (BT20), 1140lb (BT24).

Eagle-Weslake V12

'Having the privilege of making one's own mistakes is great.'

Dan Gurney

Not since 1921 had an American in an American car won a Grand Prix race in Europe. In 1967 Dan Gurney from California broke the 46-year 'duck' at Spa in the Belgian GP – but with qualifications. His Formula 1 Eagle, although backed by American dollars, and wearing American blue and white, was actually built in Britain to British designs of engine and chassis. It was an outstanding victory, nonetheless, and but for Gurney's subsequent preoccupation with the Indianapolis 500 Miles race and USAC events, might well have been followed up with further GP successes.

The Eagle was born late in 1965, when Gurney and the Texan ex-driver Carroll Shelby, with backing from Goodyear, formed AAR (for All-American Racers) Inc. at Santa Ana, California, and engaged Len Terry, designer of the Lotus 38 which won

Anglo-American Racer: the 3-litre Formula 1 Eagle designed by Len Terry and driven by Dan Gurney to victories in the Belgian GP at Spa and the Race of Champions at Brands Hatch in 1967. The 60 degree V12 Weslake engine had four overhead camshafts operating four valves per cylinder, and at its best gave around 400 bhp at 10000 rpm

that year's Indianapolis 500, to produce a new car for them. It was to be a dual-purpose design, able to contest 3-litre Formula 1 races powered by a new 12-cylinder Gurney-Weslake engine, and the Indianapolis 500 with larger Ford V8 units. The F1 cars were to be built in Britain, so a supplementary UK company called Anglo-American Racers was based at Rye, Sussex, close to cylinder head expert Harry Weslake's premises, where the F1 engine was produced, with Aubrey Woods as chief designer.

It was a compact, elegant 90 degree V12 with a bore and stroke of 72.8×60.3 mm (2997cc), and twin overhead camshafts under handsome finned covers to each bank of cylinders, operating 48 valves in all. The seven-bearing crankshaft ran in thin wall bearings, and Lucas supplied the fuel injection and transistorised ignition. The

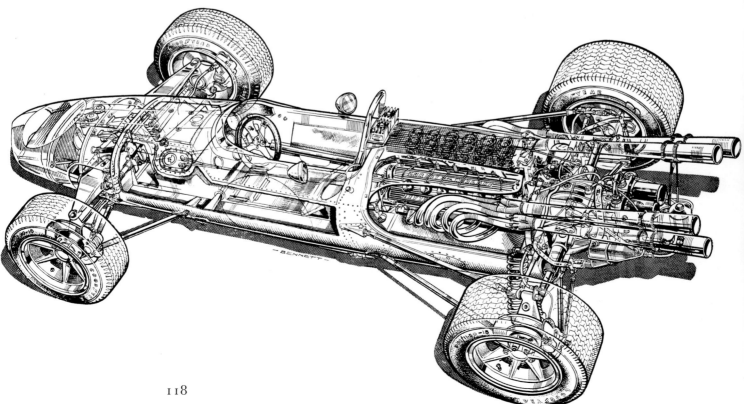

Formula 1 car (Type T1G) was of full riveted monocoque construction, broadly following Terry's Lotus 38 layout, with four steel bulkheads and fibreglass nose and tail, although the gauge of the light alloy sheeting varied according to the stresses it was to withstand. Suspension followed typical Grand Prix lines, with fabricated top links, wide-base lower wishbones, and inboard Armstrong coil spring/damper units at the front, and single top links, reversed lower wishbones and twin radius arms at the rear, with exposed coil spring/damper units. Special AAR six-spoke cast magnesium wheels were fitted, the exhausts merged into four impressive megaphones, and in all the Eagle looked a clean, purposeful design, well set off in metallic blue and white, with the nose forming a curved eagle's beak.

Completion of the V12 Gurney-Weslake engine was well behind that of the car, so Gurney had to drive his 1966 races with a 2·7-litre Inter-Continental type Coventry Climax four-cylinder engine giving under 240 bhp. Early Eagle appearances were thus simple chassis development runs, although Gurney ran seventh in the rain-soaked 1966 Belgian GP, and scored another seventh and two fifths in other races. The Weslake V12 appeared in the Italian GP at Monza, when it gave 364 bhp at 9500 rpm; but rather too intermittently. Gurney retired with engine trouble after only seven laps, vacated the US GP after 13, and in the Mexican GP, reverted to the Climax-engined car while Bob Bondurant retired the V12 after 24 laps.

Fortune was also unkind to Eagle at Indianapolis that year, when five T2G cars with 4·2-litre Ford pushrod overhead valve engines qualified at speeds between 159 mph and 162·45 mph. Gurney was eliminated in a first lap multiple shunt, and though the other Eagles all finished, the highest placed was a modest ninth despite one having held the lead at one stage. A winter's hard work down at Rye ensued, the Weslake V12 emerging for 1967 after showing 409 bhp on the brake. A second car had been completed, and the season opened brightly for AAR when Dan Gurney won the Race of Champions at Brands Hatch, beating Bandini's Ferrari. Fellow Californian Richie Ginther in the second car was third in the opening heat, and lay second to Gurney in the final when brake problems forced him out.

With the Eagle-Weslake about 150 lb over the 1100 lb minimum limit, a blitz on weight was now waged, magnesium and titanium being used wherever practical, even the bulkheads and exhaust headers being made of the latter. In all some 90 lb was saved, albeit at considerable expense. Trouble still dogged the cars at Monaco and Zandvoort, but the fuel injection was improved, claimed output rising to 417 bhp, although subsequent trials on the BRM brake at Bourne brought a top reading of only 390 bhp. Even so, Gurney's great day came in June, when he carried off the Belgian GP at Spa, always one of the year's hardest races, averaging a record 145·98 mph and leaving the lap record at 150·85 mph after an epic drive.

Dan Gurney in the imposing Formula 1 Eagle V12 during an all too brief drive in the 1967 Monaco GP; he was out after five laps with a broken fuel pump drive

Two strings to their bow: Eagle ambitions centred on the lucrative Indianapolis 500 as well as Grand Prix racing. Dan Gurney's 1966 race on the famous 'Hoosier Bowl' was woefully short, his All American Racers Eagle-Ford suffering serious damage in a monstrous lap 1 multiple shunt which eliminated 11 cars in all. Note the 'eagle's' beak nose and the multiplicity of decals characteristic of Indianapolis racing

Prospects for the rest of 1967 looked good, but fuel feed and other troubles plagued the Eagles, the worst blow coming at the Nürburgring where Gurney comfortably led the German GP when a drive shaft broke with little more than a lap between the Eagle and a second great victory. A third place in the Canadian GP was meagre compensation; the Weslake engines, suffering from imprecise 'one-off' manufacturing methods, proved increasingly erratic and brittle, and Gurney decided to take over assembly himself at a factory in Ashford, Kent. This proved equally unsuccessful, and after three dispirited 1968 performances Gurney switched to a McLaren-Ford for the final three Grands Prix, and then announced his retirement from Formula 1 in order to concentrate on American USAC and other events.

A Terry-designed Indianapolis Eagle never won the 500 outright, but Gurney lay second in 1967 until a valve in his special Weslake-modified, production-based Ford Fairlane unit burned out, while 'rookie' Denny Hulme in another Eagle placed fourth. Then Gurney won the Rex Mays 300 Miles at Riverside, and in 1968 the lanky Californian took a hard-earned second place at Indianapolis, headed only by Bobby Unser in a newer Eagle with turbo-supercharged Offenhauser engine.

Though much missed in the Grand Prix world, All-American Racers and Eagle had firmly arrived.

Specification
Engine
Gurney-Weslake 60 degree V12; bore and stroke, 72·8 × 60·3mm; capacity, 2997cc; four overhead camshafts operating four valves per cylinder; Lucas fuel injection; Lucas transistorised ignition; maximum power, 370 bhp at 9500rpm, rising to a claimed 417 bhp at 10000rpm.
Transmission
Hewland DG300 five-speed gearbox in unit with ZF limited-slip differential.
Chassis
Full monocoque construction. Front suspension by top arms, lower wishbones and inboard Armstrong coil spring/damper units; rear suspension by single top links, lower wishbones and twin radius arms with Armstrong coil spring/damper units. Girling outboard disc brakes. Goodyear tyres.
Dimensions
Wheelbase, 8ft 0·5in; track, 5ft 1in front and rear; dry weight, 1280lb, reducing to 1196lb.

Lotus-Ford 49

'The Lotus is a completely scientific study. Colin Chapman is a fine designer.'

Enzo Ferrari

Until the late 1950s, Grand Prix cars were *complete* cars, with engines, gearboxes, suspension and chassis all produced in the one factory. Coopers of Surbiton changed all that when they adopted the Coventry Climax engine, and what is often slightingly called 'the Formula 1 kit car' was born. Apart from Ferrari, and BRM, the use of proprietary power units, transmissions etc, has become the norm, and bewailers of 'lost pedigrees' can only take comfort in the fact that, without such 'over the counter' amenities, Britain would scarcely stand where she does in modern Grand Prix racing.

When Coventry Climax, having faithfully served a clamorous motor racing world for 10 strenuous years, and produced 86 F1 victories, decided to pull out after 1965, they precipitated a major crisis among the British teams. Cooper turned to Maserati for engines, Brabham to Repco, while Lotus made do with 1965 Climax V8s 'Tasmanised' to 2 litres pending arrival of the BRM H16 unit. When that came, it proved lamentably down on dependability and up on weight, so that Lotus's 1966 achievements looked decidedly meagre after their sweeping Championship

'double' the previous year. Yet 'kingpin' Colin Chapman was neither surprised nor notably depressed; once again he had a card up his sleeve.

Lotus involvement with the Ford Motor Company had increased progressively ever since the evolution of the twin-cam Lotus-Ford engine in 1961, with the Indianapolis exploits and the special Lotus-Cortina road car among the highlights. At the same time Cosworth Engineering, the company formed by two Lotus ex-employees, Mike Costin and Keith Duckworth, had successfully developed first an Anglia-based Formula Junior engine and then a Cortina-based single-cam F2 unit. Their next aim was a new engine with Cortina block for the 1600cc Formula 2 beginning in 1967, but meantime Colin Chapman had persuaded the very competition-minded Ford company at Dagenham to sponsor the production of a 3-litre Formula 1 unit. It was agreed that a 'pilot' 1600cc four-cylinder F2 engine with twin-cam four-valve head on a Cortina base should be built first, and that the F1 engine would use two such cylinder blocks, with reduced stroke, on a common crankcase.

Antipodean race followers saw and heard the new Lotus-Ford in the 1967–68 winter, when Jim Clark took out a Formula 1 car designated 49T with engine reduced to $2\frac{1}{2}$ litres for the Tasman series

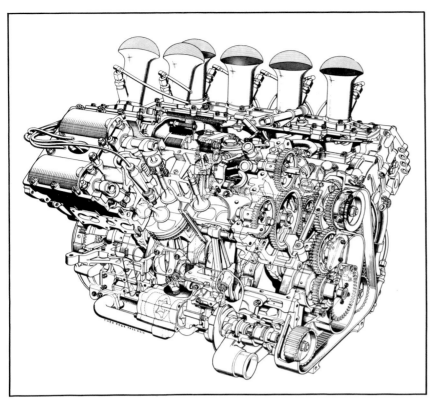

points to the aft end of a monocoque body nacelle made in 18swg light alloy with mild steel bulkheads. The forward bulkhead supported the front suspension, while triangulated tubular subframes bolted to the back of the engine block supported the rear suspension, with the radius arms picking up on the monocoque. Transmission was through a ZF five-speed gearbox, and the entire engine and transmission was left exposed. Cosworth had spared no effort in making their engine occupy as small a space as possible, with oil and water pumps and other auxiliaries all tucked neatly away within its dimensions, while in complement Chapman and Phillippe kept frontal area to a minimum with a typically clean hull on which the usual Lotus inboard front coil springs with rocking-arm top wishbones featured.

The DFV cylinder dimensions were markedly oversquare at 85·7 × 64·8mm, and designer Keith Duckworth's aim of exceeding 400bhp was realised with a steady brake reading of 408bhp at 9000rpm. The five-

DFV for Victory: Ford's new Cosworth-designed Formula 1 engine quickly put new fire into British Grand Prix efforts, beginning brilliantly with victory first time out in Lotus's new 49 at Zandvoort in the 1967 Dutch GP. The 90 degree V8 unit has four overhead camshafts, four valves per cylinder, and gave an initial 408 bhp at 9000 rpm. Ten years later the same engine is giving 435 bhp, and has won close on 100 Championship GPs

Cosworth thus committed themselves to producing two important new engines for £100000 while Lotus's new chief designer, Maurice Phillipe, got down with Colin Chapman to the task of designing a new car around the F1 Cosworth-Ford unit. A mock-up of this DFV engine with all ancillaries was sent to the new Hethel works to which Lotus had just moved, with delivery of the first real engine promised for May 1967. Meantime Lotus had signed up Graham Hill as driver alongside Jim Clark, and when the first Lotus-Ford 49 was ready, it was Hill who did all the early testing and setting-up.

The 49 evolved from the 1966 BRM 16-cylinder engined Type 43, with the DFV a major load-bearer, being bolted at four

Right: front suspension detail on the 49, showing the top rocker arm, lower wishbone, Armstrong inboard coil spring/damper unit, and outboard brake with drilled disc for lightness and heat dissipation

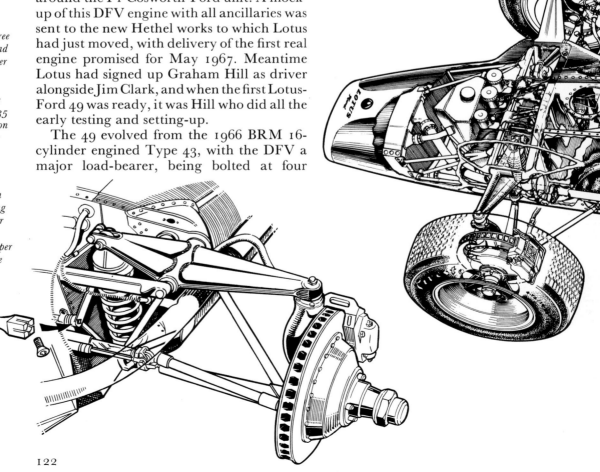

Above: *the Lotus 49 very
conveniently 'came apart'
for maintenance when the
engine was removed*

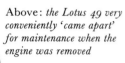

The Lotus 49 ghosted to
show disposition of major
components; the Cosworth-
Ford engine formed a load-
bearing member, supporting
the rear suspension and
gearbox subframe in con-
junction with the monocoque
centre section to which it
was bolted. A five-speed ZF
gearbox was used in the
first season, replaced in
1968 by a Hewland unit

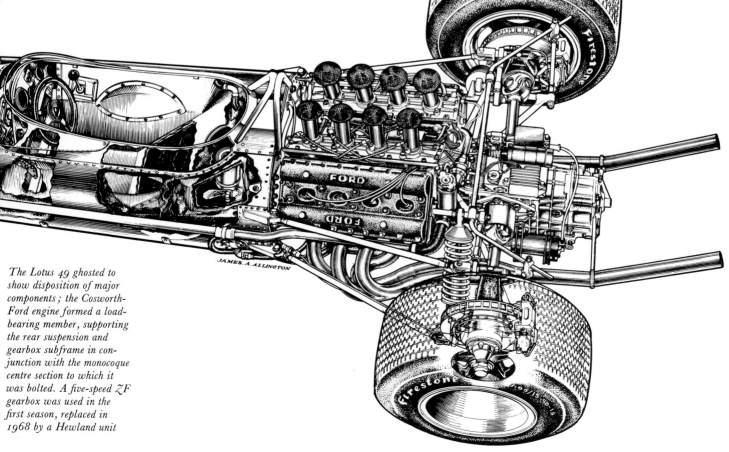

1968 was the year of the aerofoil, foreshadowed by Colin Chapman's 'wedge' engine cover on the Lotus 49B. Here Graham Hill scores his fifth victory in the Monaco GP

Two high-winged Lotus 49s in battle during the 1968 Mexican GP. Race winner Hill's car wears the Gold Leaf Team Lotus livery of red and gold, while Jo Siffert's car carries Rob Walker's dark blue colours

bearing crankshaft ran in Vandervell 'thin wall' shell bearings, Lucas transistorised electronic ignition and Lucas port fuel injection was employed, and the sparking plugs were 10mm Autolite of Ford manufacture. Power flow in the middle revs range was initially erratic, coming in with a disconcerting surge at around 6500rpm, but this problem went unsolved on the Lotus 49's first race appearance, the Dutch GP at Zandvoort on June 4th, 1967. Hill boosted

Hethel and Dagenham morale by making the fastest lap in practice, but retired from the race after 11 laps with broken timing gear. Then Clark moved into the lead on lap 17, to score a truly euphoric victory for an all-new design by over 20 seconds from Brabham's Repco-Brabham.

Through the rest of that season the 49 proved itself the year's fastest F1 car, although not the most reliable. Problems of erratic throttle response and over-cool brakes

being ironed out, and sundry refinements effected, it won four more GPs that year, the British, US, Mexican and the non-Championship Spanish event, all falling to Jim Clark. That incomparable driver then opened 1968 by winning the South African GP, but lost his life in a tragic Formula 2 race at Hockenheim. Graham Hill rallied the stricken Lotus team by winning the Spanish, Monaco and Mexican GPs with the improved 49B, which now had a Hewland gearbox in place of the ZF, the wheelbase lengthened by 3in, and a power increase to 415bhp; the car also grew, first a wedge tail and then wings which though aesthetically offensive were aerodynamically effective. Hill's successes gained him his second World Drivers' Championship, while the Swiss Jo Siffert's victory in the British GP with private entrant Rob Walker's 49 added to Hill's wins clinched the Manufacturers' Championship for Lotus as well.

In 1968 Lotus lost the exclusive use of the remarkable Cosworth DFV engine, Ford making it available to other British teams at an initial price of £7500. The gallant 49 soldiered on into 1970, winning 13 GPs in all, plus six Tasman races with a special 49T 2½-litre version. As for the Cosworth-Ford engine, this has since won nearly 100 Grands Prix, but it was in the Lotus 49 that it first achieved race-worthiness and won its first epoch-making victories.

Specification

Engine
Cosworth-Ford DFV 90 degree V8; bore and stroke, 85·7 × 64·8mm, capacity, 2993cc; four overhead camshafts, two per bank, operating four valves per cylinder; Lucas port fuel injection; Lucas transistorised ignition; maximum power, 408bhp at 9000rpm, rising to 415bhp at 9500rpm in 1968, and eventually to 430bhp at 10000rpm in 1969-70.

Transmission
Lotus-ZF five-speed gearbox in 1967; Hewland five-speed box, 1968-70.

Chassis
Truncated monocoque with front suspension sub-frame, and load-bearing power unit. Front suspension by Armstrong inboard coil spring/damper units and wishbones; rear suspension by single top link, reversed lower wishbones, twin radius arms and Armstrong coil spring/damper units. Girling outboard disc brakes. Firestone tyres.

Dimensions
Wheelbase, 7ft 11in in 1967, 8ft 2in in 1968-70; front track, 5ft in 1967, 5ft 2·5in 1968-70; rear track, 5ft 1in; dry weight, 1102lb in 1967, 1180lb in 1968, 1190lb in 1969-70.

Matra-Ford

'Thanks to racing, Matra is known the world over.'

Jean-Luc Lagardère

The success and availability of the Cosworth-Ford DFV V8 engine was an immense relief to Formula 1 constructors. British teams adopted it one after another, and even the chauvinist French un-bent so far as to employ the engine in a shrewd piece of Franco-British compromise which brought the name Matra right into the limelight. SA Engins Matra is a large concern which manufactures exotic electronic equipment, space missiles and satellites, and a variety of other products. The name derives from Mecanique-Aviation-Traction, their former company title, and it was as suppliers of fibreglass that they were plunged willy-nilly into motor manufacture, by taking over Réné Bonnet's small sports car company as creditors in 1964. Matra swiftly developed racing ambitions, and by 1965 were in Formula 3 with a very neat little monocoque. Two years later they emerged as European Formula 2 Champions, thanks to the two-car team of Cosworth-engined cars managed by Ken Tyrrell and driven by Jacky Ickx and Jackie Stewart.

That year Matra secured a long-term loan from the French Government of 6 million francs (about £0.75 million) to build an all-French Formula 1 car with 3-litre 12-cylinder engine. On this project they eagerly sought the services of Ken Tyrrell and Jackie Stewart who, while very interested in having a Formula 1 Matra chassis, had greater confidence in the race-proved Cosworth-Ford DFV V8 than in a new and undeveloped Matra V12. An apparent *impasse* was admirably solved when two one-car teams were formed for 1968, one by Matra Sports using the 100 per cent French Matra V12 with Jean-Pierre Beltoise as driver, the other by Matra International, using a Matra-Cosworth with Stewart as driver and Tyrrell as manager. Both teams were supported by the French Elf Petroleum group, which was even newer to motor racing than Matra but equally keen to exploit its publicity in the world of motor sport.

Although at least 420bhp was expected from Matra's 12-cylinder power unit, the all-French car was heavier than the first

The French Matra MS80 with Cosworth-Ford V8 engine in which Jackie Stewart won the 1969 World Championship. Embodying the design sophistications of a manufacturer with exotic aerospace and missile connections, it nevertheless followed the basic British formula, and with a top rate driver, team manager and organisation, achieved success

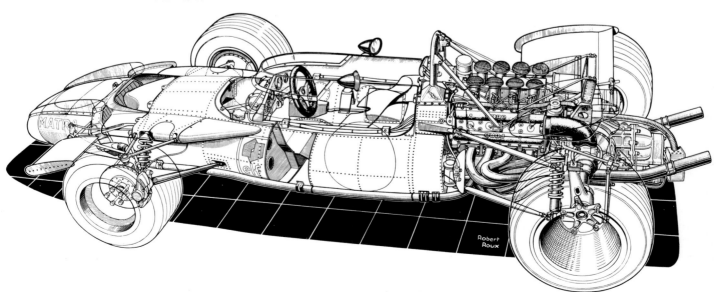

Cosworth-engined car, the MS10, while J-P Beltoise, although a fighter, had a defective right arm and lacked the sheer genius of a Stewart. The Anglo-French version was, indeed, the best bet, as 1968 and 1969 proved. The cars were built at Matra-Sports' new headquarters at Velizy, Paris, and full use was made of computers and other specialist Matra facilities in designing them. As one basic chassis had to serve for two different engines, the MS10 could not exploit the Cosworth DFV's advantage of bearing chassis loads, a subframe being attached to the Matra monocoque. This was a most professional structure, as befitted a product of France's aerospace experts, while, instead of employing rubber 'bag' fuel tanks, the monocoque itself embodied side pontoons forming compartmented metal tanks, with bulkheads giving maximum rigidity, and all joins sealed with a polymer resin. This was aeronautical practice, tricky to achieve but valuable in weight-saving. Suspension followed current fashion, the front coil spring/damper units being shrouded in the bodywork and operated by rocker arms; outboard disc brakes were used and the tyres were Dunlop.

Matra International's debut with the very new MS10 came in the 1968 Race of Champions at Brands Hatch, where Stewart finished sixth. Unfortunately he damaged his right wrist in a subsequent Formula 2 race at a crucial period in MS10 development, but Beltoise drove the car in the Spanish GP, leading for four laps when an oil filter seal defected. The Frenchman lost four places, but set the fastest lap in his fight back on the leader board. Stewart had returned, his

wrist in a plastic sleeve, for the Belgian GP, but this time the car suffered fuel feed troubles when leading, forcing the plucky Scot back to fourth place. But he won his next race, the Dutch GP, in the rain, with Beltoise's V12 Matra second, recording the best performance by French cars for many years. Three Grands Prix later and Stewart scored an epic victory at the Nürburgring, winning the German GP by over four minutes in heavy rain and fog which restricted visibility at some points to 50 yards.

Snatching a weekend to win the non-Championship Gold Cup race at Oulton Park, Stewart then went to Monza where his Cosworth engine blew up, ran sixth in the Canadian GP, scored another great win in the US GP, and then lost his World Championship chances through a fuel blockage in the decisive Mexican GP finale. Ironically the blockage was caused through a particle of the polymer resin tank sealant working loose. Stewart having lost the driver title to Graham Hill, and Matra the Constructors' Cup to Lotus, both began the 1969 season in determined mood. While Jackie Stewart was winning the opening round in South Africa with an MS10, the Velizy works were busy completing an improved car, the MS80. Designed by Bernard Boyer, this had an improved monocoque of rather bloated appearance, but skilfully concentrating fuel weight centrally. The DFV engine now served as the stressed member for which it was designed, and gave an extra 500rpm and 15bhp. Inboard rear brakes were fitted to reduce unsprung weight, but the front coil spring/damper units were transferred to an outboard position, an apparent reversion which, in fact, simplified the action, reduced weight and cooled the dampers more effectively. A second Cosworth-engined car was now run by Matra International, driven by J-P Beltoise whose V12 F1 car was withdrawn for 12 months for more development.

Stewart's first race in the MS80 was the Brands Hatch Race of Champions, where the car proved considerably better than the MS10, with a more rigid chassis and none of its understeer, thanks to suspension changes. Stewart won the race, then went to Barcelona and scored again in the Spanish GP. This was the last race in which wings of free dimensions were allowed, these appendages thereafter being of restricted size and attached to the car proper rather than the suspension. At Silverstone the irrepressible Scot put in some more practice by winning the International Trophy, but suffered a broken drive shaft at Monaco. He won again at Zandvoort in the Dutch GP, however, then repeated the act in the French GP at Clermont-Ferrand, with Beltoise second in another French-blue Matra to the great joy of the crowd. Stewart made it three in a row by carrying off the British GP at Silverstone, then scored a second in the German GP and yet another first in the Italian GP, worthily clinching the 1969 World Championship titles both for himself and for Matra. Six Grand Prix victories plus two lesser wins was a fine achievement, especially by a marque in only its second year of Formula 1. Although Matra subsequently tried extremely hard

The French greatly approved Stewart's victory with the Matra in their colours at Clermont-Ferrand in the 1969 French GP, especially when team mate J-P Beltoise in another Matra-Ford followed home in second place. From this aspect the neat location of the rear aerofoil above the engine can be seen, also the fins on the nose and distinctive fairings over the outrigged front suspension pivots

with their glorious-sounding V12, they never repeated the Ford-engined MS80's wonderful 1969 season.

Specification
Engine
Cosworth-Ford DFV 90 degree V8; bore and stroke, 85·7 × 64·8mm; capacity, 2993cc; four overhead camshafts, two per bank, operating four valves per cylinder; Lucas fuel injection; Lucas transistorised ignition; max power, 415bhp at 9500rpm in 1968, rising to 430bhp at 10000 in 1969.
Transmission
Hewland five-speed gearbox in unit with ZF limited-slip differential.
Chassis
Truncated monocoque with integral fuel tanks. Front suspension by wishbones and Armstrong inboard coil spring/damper units on 1968 MS10; outboard units on MS80 in 1969. Rear suspension by top links, reversed lower wishbones and twin radius arms, with Armstrong coil spring/damper units. Girling ventilated disc brakes, outboard on MS10 in 1968, outboard front, inboard rear on MS80 in 1969. Dunlop tyres.
Dimensions
Wheelbase, 7ft 11·2in (MS10), 7ft 10·5in (MS80); track, front and rear, 4ft 9·9in (MS10), 5ft 3in (MS80); dry weight, 1240lb (MS10), 1178lb (MS80).

BRM P160

'And if a house be divided against itself, that house cannot stand.'

Luke ii. 17

Since 1949 the ever-keen but trouble-fraught BRM concern had tried V16s, big fours, V8s and H16s, with mixed results ranging from the nadir of their early 16-cylinder efforts to the zenith of their 1962 World Championship. With its two crankshafts and duplicated auxiliaries, the 1966 3-litre H16 had proved disappointingly heavy, unreliable and down on power compared with the rival Cosworth-Ford, so for 1967 BRM tried a V12 for Formula 1. This was a 60 degree four-cam unit originally designed for sports car racing, and giving about 360 bhp at 9800 rpm. Bore and stroke were 74·7 × 57·2 mm (2998cc), the seven-bearing crankshaft ran in Vandervell thin wall bearings, and the camshafts were driven by roller chain. After H16 complexities, the Bourne team's priorities were lightness, simplicity and reliability, one aim being to sell the new engine to other teams. As things transpired, since BRM themselves were still using the H16s, just such a team, McLaren, became the first users of the V12.

The McLaren-BRM first appeared in the Canadian GP at Mosport, where driver/manufacturer Bruce McLaren went encouragingly well until a flat battery robbed him of second place. The Bourne gremlins then settled in to spoil the rest of his season, and while the New Zealander changed to

Cosworth power for 1968 the V12 went into BRM's own new car, the P126, and also to the Cooper team. The P126 was designed and built by Len Terry, who had produced Dan Gurney's F1 Eagle. Indeed, this BRM was virtually an improved Eagle, but smaller as it was not required to serve both as an Indianapolis and F1 car, and using up various parts already made up for the abortive BRM H16. It had a twin-pontoon, four bulkhead monocoque with a subframe to support the rear suspension and engine, which was not designed for stress-bearing. Like the Eagle, the suspension was 'standard Formula 1' all round, the front springs being inboard in unit with Dutch Koni coaxial hydraulic dampers.

While Terry was laying down the P126, BRM decided to run a 2½-litre version with shortened stroke in the Tasman race series early in 1968 as a means of 'sorting' the new design before serious Grand Prix work began. Lotus and Jim Clark happened to be out there too, with a 2·5-litre Cosworth-engined Type 49T, but McLaren with the BRM beat Clark to win the Teretonga race in heavy rain, giving an encouraging start to the career of the P126. Back in Europe, however, the 'BRM blight' soon set in. Drivers Graham Hill and Jackie Stewart had left in 1967, and the team next lost Mike Spence when he

The modern look: the Yardley-BRM P160 poses against a wall, showing the economy of size, the huge wheels, slender nose and big rear wing typical of the Grand Prix car of the early 1970s

Champions all: Scotsman
Jackie Stewart, worthy
successor to Jim Clark,
became World Champion
in 1969 with the Matra-
Ford (above) and in 1971
with the Tyrrell-Ford
(right), when each make
won the Manufacturers'
title. The Matra MS80,
seen winning the 1969
Dutch GP, was designed by
Bernard Boyer, built at
Velizy, Paris, around the
Cosworth-Ford DFV V8
engine, and raced under the
management of Ken
Tyrrell. The Tyrrell 003,
seen winning the 1971
German GP with new cold
air box atop the DFV's fuel
injection, was designed by
Derek Gardner and built
at East Horsley

Close-up of the P160 in 1971 form with the nose removed, laying bare the forward bulkhead, radiator and plumbing; the outboard coil spring/damper units of the front suspension can also be seen. This is the car with which Jo Siffert won the Austrian GP at Osterreich-ring

Opposite, top: Aerodynamic variations on Jo Siffert's 1971 P160 at Monza, where it is running without nose aerofoils. It has a 'chisel' nose, and the ribs supplementing the end plates on the rear wing can be clearly seen

BRM's V12 36-valve engine gave over 400 bhp in its best years; the roll-over hoop support stays are bolted to the cylinder heads

Opposite, lower: this photograph of Jackie Oliver in the Race of Champions emphasises the formidable frontal area offered by modern tyres, and also shows the broad-based triangular form of the monocoque

crashed fatally in a Lotus at Indianapolis. The works made sundry detail changes to the Terry P126, which then emerged as the P133, to be driven by Dick Attwood into second place at Monaco, and by Pedro Rodriguez into second place at Spa. These were its sole achievements, however, the engine suffering persistent lubrication troubles and being at least 20 bhp down on the opposition.

The next year brought the P138, which had new four-valve heads with the induction system moved outside and the exhaust centralised, a lighter BRM gearbox in place

Below: *Hethel V8s:*
Brazilian driver Emerson
Fittipaldi with the
trendsetting Lotus 72 with
Cosworth-Ford V8 engine,
during the 1971 German
GP at Nürburgring. The

following year he won the
World Drivers' Champion-
ship after victories in the
Spanish, Belgian, British,
Austrian and Italian GPs
with the 72 (see page 137)

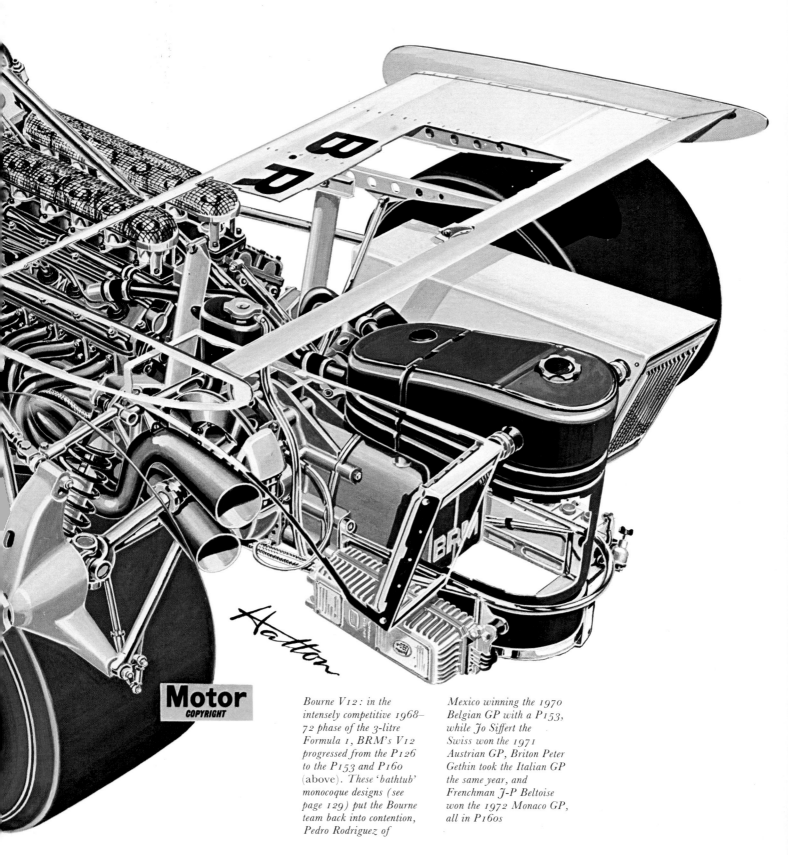

Bourne V12: in the intensely competitive 1968–72 phase of the 3-litre Formula 1, BRM's V12 progressed from the P126 to the P153 and P160 (above). These 'bathtub' monocoque designs (see page 129) put the Bourne team back into contention, Pedro Rodriguez of Mexico winning the 1970 Belgian GP with a P153, while Jo Siffert the Swiss won the 1971 Austrian GP, Briton Peter Gethin took the Italian GP the same year, and Frenchman J-P Beltoise won the 1972 Monaco GP, all in P160s

of the Hewland, and a modified monocoque, but all to no avail. A lightened version, the P139, then appeared, but driver John Surtees was not amused when the suspension failed on the first lap of the British GP. His departure from the team after six retirements and one third place in the US GP, preceded by that of chief engineer Tony Rudd, left team morale very low indeed. For 1970 Louis Stanley, husband of Sir Alfred Owen's sister Jean, became BRM chairman and sponsorship by the Yardley perfume concern was arranged. Tim Parnell was appointed team manager, and two ex-Eagle employees, Aubrey Woods and Tony Southgate, joined as engine and chassis designers respectively.

Their joint new product, the Yardley-BRM P153, had a 'bathtub' type monocoque with bulbous Matra-style 'pregnant' side sponsons, occupied by two 23-gallon fuel tanks of rubberised fabric, as required by 1970 FIA regulations. The engine, still in a tubular subframe, was much revised by Woods who at once reverted to pre-1969 port arrangements with the exhausts outside the vee and the inlets and injectors within it. Larger valves, improved cooling and other modifications brought a healthier output of about 425 bhp, while suspension revisions included outboard coil spring/damper units at the front and much use of titanium. The body had a new 'shovel nose' in fibreglass, and with this handsome car the fiery little Mexican driver Pedro Rodriguez brought BRM right out of the doldrums by scoring a resounding start-to-finish victory at 149·9 mph in the 1970 Belgian GP. But for the P153's unexpectedly high fuel consumption he would surely have won the US GP as well, for he was leading with but seven laps to go when he had to stop for fuel, letting Fittipaldi's Lotus past.

Southgate's next effort, the P160 of 1971, was a logical development of the P153. The roadholding was now exceptionally good, and in conjunction with 435 bhp and an ability to rev to 11500 rpm, a new nose which reduced drag and improved stability, and inboard rear brakes, the car was highly competitive if still of doubtful reliability. Overheating, gear linkage and oil pressure problems contributed to too many retirements, as did ignition failure through vibration affecting the coil, bolted on the rollover bar. But the P160 won three times in 1971; Rodriguez took the Rothmans' International Trophy race at Oulton Park, Swiss driver Jo Siffert had his day of glory in the Austrian GP at Osterreichring, being fastest in practice, uncatchable in the race, and

making fastest lap as well, while Peter Gethin won a hair-raising Italian GP at Monza by pipping three other cars at the very post. Gethin was also leading the distressing Rothman's 'Victory' race at Brands Hatch when it was stopped following the fatal accident to Siffert which so sadly ended the season.

Yardley sponsorship of BRM stopped that year, and was taken over in 1972 by Marlboro. Next variant in the long list of racing cars from Bourne was the unsuccessful P180, but the P160 was to figure again in what proved to be BRM's last outright Formula 1 wins. These were the 1972 Monaco GP, when the Frenchman J-P Beltoise put up an inspired drive to lead a rain-soaked race from beginning to end, and the John Player Victory meeting at Brands Hatch, where Beltoise again won. Sadly the team's fighting spirit eroded thereafter as reliability and performance diminished. A P201 followed the P180, after which the Stanley-BRM ran an abbreviated and unsuccessful 1975 season. Following a year's retirement the team introduced the new P207 for 1977 with sponsorship from Rotary Watches.

Specification
Engine
60 degree V12 BRM; bore and stroke, 74·7 × 57·2 mm; capacity, 2998 cc; four overhead camshafts, two per bank, operating two valves per cylinder in 1967–68; four valves per cylinder from 1969; Lucas indirect fuel injection; Lucas transistorised ignition; max power, 360 bhp at 9800 rpm in 1967, rising to 460 bhp at 11000 rpm in 1974.
Transmission
Hewland five-speed gearbox in unit with ZF limited-slip differential in 1968, BRM five-speed box from 1969 on.
Chassis
Truncated monocoque with tubular sub-frame for engine and rear suspension. Front suspension by wishbones and inboard coil spring/ Koni damper units, 1968–69; outboard 1970 on. Rear suspension by single top link, lower wishbones, radius arms and outboard coil spring/ Koni damper units. Girling-BRM disc brakes, inboard at rear on p160, 1971; Dunlop tyres to 1969; Firestone 1970–74; Goodyear 1975.
Dimensions
Wheelbase, 8 ft; front track, 5 ft; rear track, 4 ft 11 in; Formula weight, 1210 lb.

Lotus-Ford 72

'While other manufacturers advance step by step Chapman alone dares to go forward in leaps and bounds . . .'

José Rosinski, 'Automobile Year'

If the Grand Prix cars of the mid-1970s all looked pretty much alike, it was scarcely surprising when so many used the faithful V8 Cosworth-Ford DFV engine and Hewland gearbox. Yet someone had to set the pattern, and just as the genius of Colin Chapman pointed the way with his Lotus 25 in 1962 and the 49 in 1967, so the Type 72 of 1970 was yet another trendsetter for others to copy. Destined to race far longer than intended, this car had an exhausting career lasting six seasons, during which it won 19 GPs and four non-Championship F1 races, and gained two World Drivers' Championships and three Constructors' titles.

The most obvious novelties of the Lotus 72, when it was unveiled in April 1970, were the side radiators, chisel nose and inboard front and rear brakes, but other subtleties lurked in a design produced by Maurice Phillippe, former aircraft engineer, under Colin Chapman's guidance. Undoubtedly, the Lotus 56 turbine-powered Indianapolis Lotus and the four-wheel-drive Type 63 with wedge shape and inboard front brakes helped inspire the new design. No nose radiator meant better air penetration and less wind resistance, aerodynamic gains further exploited by the care-

fully profiled wedge bodywork with flush-riveted external surfaces. The two side radiators were housed in fibreglass ducts, well contoured to ensure maximum airflow, and dispensing with the usual mess of plumbing from the front. Two flush NACA ducts admitted cooling air to the inboard front brakes, and two moulded 'funnels' over the discs discharged the heat generated. The brake discs were carried on live shafts with constant-velocity joints, the main aim being less unsprung weight.

A three-tier rear wing and the neat radiator pods made the bodywork of the 72 refreshingly different, although the modern tailless back end presented the customary mechanical clutter of gearbox, oil tank, oil cooler, etc., aesthetically deplorable but excellent for access and cooling. Beneath the bright red and white Players' Gold Leaf finish were further surprises. Chapman and Phillippe dispensed with coil springs for the suspension, resorting to torsion bars as pioneered by Dr Porsche on the Auto Union. Lotus's longitudinal application was beautifully compact, the springing being 'compounded' by using a torsion bar splined within a torsion tube, each combined unit being only 25in long. There

'New boy' to the Lotus team, Emerson Fittipaldi took second place in the Austrian GP and third in both the French and British GPs (seen here) of 1971

Trasversale triumphant: epitomising the modern 3-litre Formula 1 car at the peak of design sophistication, the Ferrari 312T with transverse five-speed gearbox proved a worthy mount for 1975 World Champion Niki Lauda. Water radiators for the flat-12 four-cam engine are housed within the monocoque just behind the front wheels, and there are angled oil coolers just ahead of the rear wheels and a special oil cooler for the gearbox in the rear wing mounting. Many castings and forgings produced in the Maranello foundry figure in the design

Opposite: a highly eventful 1976 season saw Lauda in the latest 312T-2 emerge as close runner-up in the World Drivers' Championship, but the marque Ferrari won the Manufacturers' Championship for the second successive year. With the high airbox above the engine banned in 1976, the car embodied waist-high air intakes in the double-skinned cockpit surround

was adjustment for ride height, and spring rates were varied by using different inner torsion bars.

The Cosworth-Ford DFV, giving about 440 bhp at 10000 rpm, drove through a Hewland DG300 five-speed gearbox. Magnesium and other light alloys featured in parts such as the hub carriers and disc brake centres, keeping overall weight close to the 530kg (1172lb) FIA minimum. A few weeks of arduous 'sorting' passed before the 72 became raceworthy. First time out, for the 1970 Spanish GP at Jarama, number one driver Jochen Rindt had the bolts on one inboard front brake shear in practice, then suffered ignition failure in the race. In the BRDC International Trophy at Silverstone and the Belgian GP at Spa the cars failed again, but Chapman and his men persevered, making diverse design 'mods' until sweet compensation came fourth time out at Zandvoort, where 'tiger' Rindt just galloped away to win the Dutch GP. He followed up with three more intoxicating victories in the

French, British and German GPs, but his winning spell broke in the Austrian GP when his engine 'let go'.

At Monza for the Italian GP a new recruit from Formula Ford and Formula 3, the young Brazilian Emerson Fittipaldi, joined the team, only to crash his new 72 in practice and non-start. Much worse befell Gold Leaf Team Lotus when Rindt, too, crashed in practice under braking from very high speed, striking the Armco barrier at a corner and being killed instantly. Poor Rindt's points score up to that race was sufficient to earn him the posthumous title of World Champion for 1970, while Lotus gained the Constructors' Cup under circumstances immeasurably bitter for the Hethel team. They missed the Canadian GP, but rallied in time for the US GP at Watkins Glen, where Fittipaldi found himself elevated to number one driver. Like Graham Hill after the death of Jim Clark in 1968, he gave the depressed Lotus team a much needed fillip by winning the $50000 race, with the Swede Reine

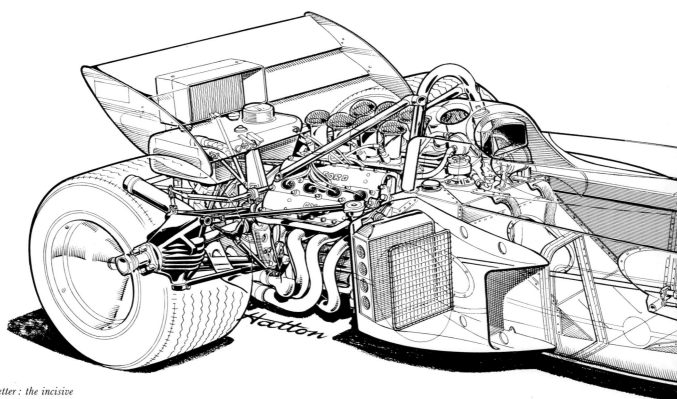

Trendsetter: the incisive wedge form of the Lotus-Ford 72 and its side-mounted radiators set a pattern in 1970 which others were soon obliged to follow. The discharge vents for the inboard front brakes on the nose can be seen

Wisell third in another Lotus Type 72.

After reaching both the heights and depths of fortune in 1970, the team had a curiously flat 1971, in which they won not a single Grand Prix. The Type 72 was still the most advanced Formula 1 car, even though its side radiators and inboard front brakes were already being copied, and a reinvigorated team emerged in 1972 as 'John Player Specials' (abbreviated to JPS) in smart black and gold decor. The three-tier rear wing had given way to a single wing set further back

and there were numerous unseen refinements. In that season Fittipaldi 'came good' to the satisfying extent of five rousing wins in the GPs of Spain, Belgium, Britain, Austria and Italy, plus four non-Championship events at Brands Hatch (twice), Silverstone and Vallelunga, Rome. The 25-year-old Brazilian became the youngest World Champion ever, while Lotus took their fifth Constructors' Championship.

In 1973 Chapman exchanged one Swedish driver, Wisell, for another, Ronnie Peterson,

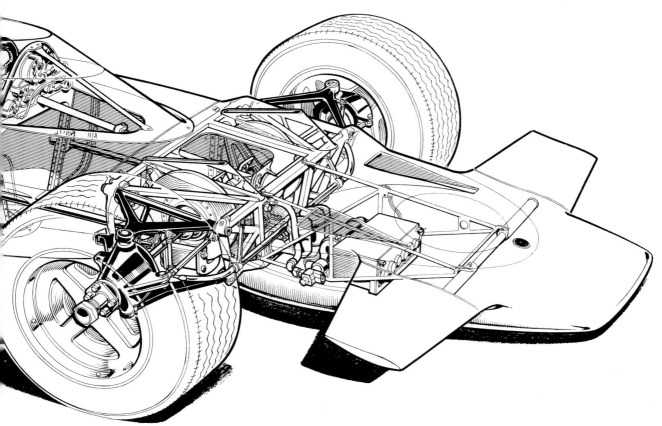

Champion's Mount: the 1976 version of the McLaren-Ford M23 with which James Hunt became World Champion (see page 156). Superbly prepared and operated by a totally professional team, powered by a Nicholson-tuned Cosworth-Ford DFV engine, and fitted with a special McLaren-developed six-speed gearbox, this four-year-old design by Gordon Coppuck won seven major GPs plus two non-Championship events in the one season

Right: Denny Hulme cornering his M23 in Yardley livery on the classic Monaco street circuit

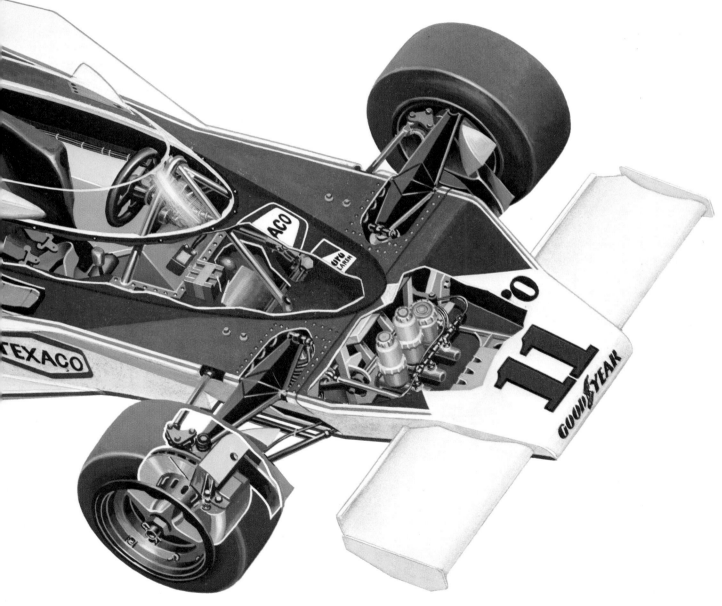

whose fire and skill inevitably meant stern rivalry with team mate Fittipaldi. The result was dramatic – no less than seven Championship race wins by JPS (three to Fittipaldi in Argentina, Brazil and Spain, and four to Peterson in France, Austria, Italy and USA) and yet another Constructors' Cup to Lotus. When Fittipaldi transferred to McLaren in 1974 Peterson was joined by the Belgian Jacky Ickx. Three GPs, the Monaco, French

and Italian, fell to the Swede and the chisel-nosed 72, while Ickx won the Brands Hatch Race of Champions.

Colin Chapman was much absorbed at this stage in Lotus production car problems, and the 72 was rather neglected. In any case it had now been around for five seasons, had endured repeated design 'mods' in efforts to restore its youth, had become notably overweight and was surely due for pensioning

Swedish driver Ronnie Peterson joined the JPS team in 1973, taking the chisel-nosed Lotus 72 to four victories in the French, Austrian, Italian and US GPs, and winning three more in 1974, when the car was in its fifth season of racing

off. But its intended successor, the 76, with novel electric clutch and 'two-pedal' control, performed indifferently, so Maurice Phillippe's old soldier was perforce dragged out for yet another year's active service.

But the opposition from Ferrari's fierce flat-12s and rival Cosworth engine users had now surpassed Lotus's 1970 concept, and with a bleak record in 1975 Hethel morale was back near rock bottom. In the JPS 72's last Championship race, the US GP which it had won in 1970 and 1973, the team could not better 14th and 19th fastest in practice and 5th and 12th in the race, eloquent of the faded glory of an outstanding Grand Prix car.

Specification
Engine
Cosworth-Ford DFV 90 degree V8; bore and stroke, 85·7 × 64·8mm, capacity, 2993cc; four overhead cam-shafts, two per bank, operating four valves per cylinder. Lucas fuel injection; Lucas transistorised ignition; maximum power, 430–440bhp at 10000rpm.
Transmission
Hewland five-speed gearbox in unit with ZF differential.
Chassis
Monocoque, with front suspension sub-frame and stress-bearing engine. Side radiators. Front suspension by wishbones and compound torsion bars; Armstrong inboard dampers. Rear suspension by triangulated wishbones and compound torsion bars; Armstrong inboard dampers. Girling inboard solid disc brakes front and rear. Firestone tyres.
Dimensions
Wheelbase, 8ft 4in; track, 4ft 9in front and rear; Formula weight, 1170lb.

The two Lotus 72s of Peterson and Fittipaldi, stripped down in the Kendall Center garage at Watkins Glen before the 1973 United States GP, won by Peterson

3-litre Tyrrell-Ford

'I had no choice. I had to build my own car.'

Ken Tyrrell

After Jackie Stewart became 1969 World Champion with the Tyrrell-entered Matra-Ford, Matra-Sports was taken over by the Chrysler-owned Simca concern. The American corporation could scarcely approve use of a Ford engine in a Grand Prix team operating under their wing, while in any case Matra themselves were eager to go 100 per cent French and employ their own V12 engine in 1970, even at risk of losing the valued services of Stewart and Tyrrell. The latter pair still considered the Cosworth-Ford V8 the better unit, and since Matra were unable to supply them with a chassis only, they had to seek elsewhere.

No McLaren, Lotus or Brabham chassis was available either, but out of the blue came an answer in the new March F1 car built at Bicester. Ken Tyrrell ordered three chassis, and Stewart raced the March in 1970, winning the Race of Champions and the Spanish GP, thanks to his own skill rather than to the car, which was deliberately of conservative design to ensure race depend-

ability. Before taking delivery, in fact, Tyrrell had realised that eventually he would have to build his own car, and thus the talented team manager from East Horsley, Surrey, became a reluctant constructor. He chose Derek Gardner, a project engineer with the Ferguson transmission company, to design the car, which was planned and built in absolute secrecy between February and August 1970.

Designated car number 001, it was a clean, simple machine with bathtub-type monocoque ending in a bulkhead to which the stress-bearing Cosworth motor was bolted. The Armstrong coil spring/damper suspension units were mounted outboard, as were the Girling front disc brakes; those at the rear were inboard, closely flanking a Hewland FG400 five-speed gearbox. A 'semi-wedge' fibreglass nose bore rather high front wings, with the radiator intake underneath, while the centre-section swelled out gracefully to house fuel cells on each side. Unsprung and overall weight were both credit-

ably low, the car scaling just 32lb above the FIA 1168lb minimum. Looking smart in blue, the new Tyrrell made its debut in the Oulton Park Gold Cup race in August 1970, when Stewart gave warning of its potential by breaking the lap record before his engine failed. He gained commanding leads in both the Canadian and US GPs before retiring, and had to vacate the Mexican GP after hitting a dog.

For 1971 the team received full sponsorship from the big French petroleum group, Elf-Aquitaine, and contested all major F1 events as Elf Team Tyrrell. Francois Cevert joined the team as number two driver, and two new cars, 002 and 003, were built, embodying numerous improvements to the monocoque, suspension and braking in the light of 1970 experience. The monocoque now terminated in a braced tubular 'hoop' which formed a sturdy roll-over bar, and provided attachment points for engine and suspension radius arms. Meantime Stewart opened the season well with 001 by placing second in the South African GP at Kyalami, then showed the new 003's formidable mettle by winning the next two Championship rounds in Spain and Monaco.

Before the French GP at Castellet Gardner had devised lofty cold air boxes – the first used on Cosworth engines – and new sports car-style wide nose fairings, to considerable aerodynamic benefit. Thus equipped, the brilliant Stewart in 003 won three GPs in a row, the French, British and German, with Cevert in the older 002 making the score one-two for Tyrrell in the French and German events. Finally Stewart gained his sixth 1971 victory in the US GP, the intoxicating overall reward being a Championship double – the drivers' title to Stewart and the constructors' to Tyrrell – in their first full season!

Clearly the Tyrrell, although epitomising the 'British standard Formula 1 kit car' of modern GP racing, had outstanding merits besides those of its drivers. Meticulous study and trial by designer Gardner of the many factors affecting performance, such as weight

1971 version of the Tyrrell-Ford. Driving car number 003 Jackie Stewart won six GPs and the World Championship titles for both himself and the car

Hatton

Innovations on the Tyrrell
007 series for 1974 included
rising rate inboard suspension, the top rocking arm
cunningly disposed to clear
inboard ventilated disc
brakes. Torsion bar rear
springing was also adopted,
but in the following season
the design reverted to
outboard front brakes and
coil springing at the rear

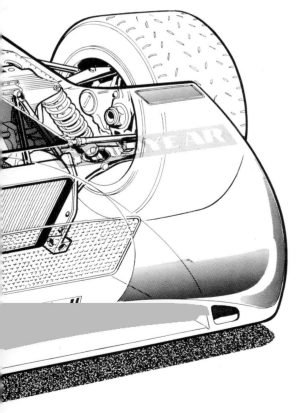

and its distribution, the aerodynamic challenge of modern wings, efficient transfer of
every last ounce of Cosworth power to the
road, and rigorous quality control in manufacture all paid dividends. Indeed, Tyrrell
standards somewhat resembled those of
Mercedes-Benz to 'mini' scale, just as Ken
Tyrrell's shrewd team control and discipline
were those of a Neubauer; it all paid off when
there were five rival teams using the same
pattern Cosworth engines, and 100ths of a
second in lap times counted.

While three new second series cars, 004,
005 and 006, were being constructed, Stewart opened 1972 in fine style by winning the
GP of Argentina in his faithful 003. Ill health
affected his form in subsequent races, but he
recovered in time to win yet again with 003
in the French GP at Clermont-Ferrand. In
the new cars the design was 'compacted',
with a 2in shorter wheelbase, stubbier full-
width nose, slab-sided monocoque and side
oil radiators faired into a neat flat deck
merging with the airbox and directing air to
the rear wing. Switching to 005, Stewart took
two races to 'shake down', and then won the
GPs of Canada and USA, becoming runner-
up to Fittipaldi in the Championship.

Again the 'wee Scot' kicked off a new season well by taking the 1973 South African GP, this time in 006. The Elf Tyrrells were then rebuilt with deformable side sections to meet new 1973 safety regulations while an extra car, 006/2, was also built. This proved immediately successful, Stewart winning the International Trophy at Silverstone, then making a grand slam in the Belgian, Monaco, Dutch and German GPs, the latter his 27th Grand Prix triumph which clinched his third Championship title. After this convincing demonstration of his prowess, Jackie Stewart retired from racing.

The season had been marred by Cevert's death at Watkins Glen, so for 1974 Tyrrell signed up the South African Jody Scheckter and Frenchman Patrick Depailler to drive the newest 007s. These had inboard front coil springing, Gardner's special dry sump pressure-lubricated Hewland gearbox, and three features first used by Lotus in 1970 – side-mounted radiators, a chisel nose and torsion bar rear suspension. After the usual early troubles the cars scored one-two in the Swedish GP, Scheckter leading home from Depailler, the South African then winning the British GP, and taking second places at Monaco and in the German GP.

In 1975 Scheckter began in 'Stewart style' by winning the South African GP, but Tyrrell fortunes thereafter tailed off. After the previous season's experience the design reverted to outboard front brakes and coil spring rear suspension, but Gardner's great surprise came late that year with his six-wheeled P34. A prime object in this bold essay was to reduce drag by using 10in diameter wheels and a narrower nose without loss of cornering or braking power, and the revolutionary 1976 Tyrrells put up some unexpectedly good performances during the season, including a highly satisfying repeat of the marque's 1974 one-two victory in the Swedish GP at Anderstorp.

Specification
Engine
Cosworth-Ford DFV 90 degree V8; bore and stroke, 85·7 × 64·8 mm, capacity, 2993cc; four overhead camshafts, two per bank, operating four valves per cylinder; Lucas fuel injection; Lucas Opus transistorised ignition; maximum power, 460bhp at 10250rpm (465bhp at 10500 in 1975).
Transmission
Hewland-Tyrrell five-speed gearbox in unit with ZF differential.
Chassis
'Bathtub' monocoque with front suspension sub-frame and 360 degrees roll 'hoop' at rear. Nose radiators on 1970-73 cars; side radiators 1974-75. Front suspension by double wishbones and outboard coil spring/damper units, 1970-75 (inboard units 1974). Rear suspension by single top links, parallel lower links, twin radius arms and outboard coil spring/damper units, 1970-75 (torsion bar rear suspension 1974). Disc brakes, inboard rear, outboard front in 1970-75 (inboard front 1974). Dunlop tyres in 1970, Goodyear tyres 1971 on.
Dimensions
Wheelbases, 7ft 10·1 to 7ft 11·7in; front track, 5ft 3in; rear track, 5ft 2·9in to 5ft 4·9in according to rim widths; Formula weight, varying from 1200 to 1275lb in 1970-72, 1348 to 1390lb in 1973-75.

Jody Scheckter in the 1975 Swedish Grand Prix

Ferrari Flat-12 312T

'It is desirable always to have 30 more horsepower than one's rivals.'

Enzo Ferrari

Apart from the fact that it is not plastered with irrelevant publicity decals and makes glorious multi-cylinder noises, a special attraction of the Grand Prix Ferrari of the 1970s decade of 'Formula 1 kit cars' is that it is a 100 per cent design entity, with engine, chassis, suspension and accoutrements all produced at Maranello. It was ironic, therefore, that at a time of tense labour relations, the great Italian marque had to buy monocoques from Britain in order to maintain their racing programme. It happened late in 1972 when Ferrari fortunes had faded badly and the British Cosworth-Ford V8-engined cars were outpacing the Italian flat-12s. Anxious to explore all design avenues but with strikes on his own doorstep, Ferrari ordered three full monocoques for a new 1973 Tipo 312-B3 series of cars from specialist John Thompson of Earls Barton, Northampton.

The cars were built, but they could not stem the flood of British success in 1973.

Their new side radiators caused overheating, while the engines had an unsatisfactory power band and were uncharacteristically unreliable. Team morale sagged and a disgruntled number one driver, Jacky Ickx, 'took a holiday'. Then Commendatore Enzo Ferrari, recovered from a spell of ill health that spring, took action. He cancelled entries for the Dutch and German GPs and made important changes in organisation and personnel at Maranello. Mauro Forghieri, brilliant former chief engineer to the racing team, was reinstated, Luca de Montezemolo was appointed team manager, and a team headed by engineers Rocchi and Bussi was formed to seek the full potential from Ferrari's splendid flat-12 48-valve engine.

Ferrari's first 180 degree engine was a $1\frac{1}{2}$-litre F1 flat-12 unit raced in 1965, after which they built a 2-litre prototype version and won the 1969 European Mountain Championship. The first 3-litre 'Boxer' Ferrari came in 1970, thrusting rudely into

Scoring his third successive first place in 1975, Niki Lauda winning the Swedish GP at Anderstorp in the Ferrari 312T. He added the French and US GPs to emerge a deserving World Champion

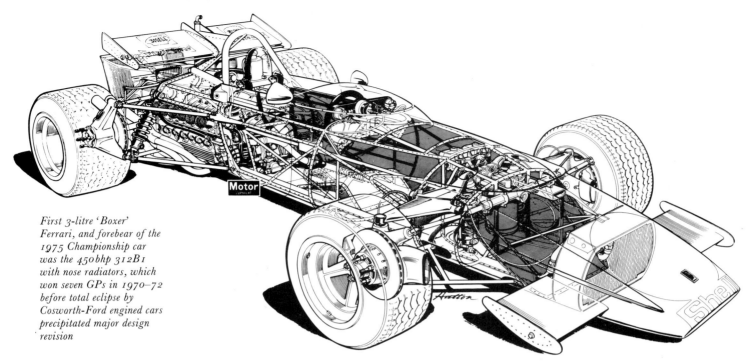

First 3-litre 'Boxer' Ferrari, and forebear of the 1975 Championship car was the 450 bhp 312B1 with nose radiators, which won seven GPs in 1970–72 before total eclipse by Cosworth-Ford engined cars precipitated major design revision

480 bhp laid bare – the flat-12 engine of one of the 312-B3/74 Ferraris removed after a practice session at Nürburgring before the 1974 German GP. Lauda took pole starting position only to crash on lap 1 but Clay Reggazoni won after holding a race-long lead

what looked like becoming 'the Cosworth age' by winning four Grands Prix. It won two more in 1971, one in 1972, and none in 1973, when the extensive redesign was in progress. Rocci and colleagues extracted over 475 bhp, but still sought improved torque most of the way up the engine's impressive 13000 rpm peak limit (on a two-roller, two-plain bearing crankshaft), and diverse radiator and wing arrangements were tried out on the Thompson nacelles during the remainder of the season.

Meanwhile a new monocoque was evolved at Maranello for the 1974 car, designated the 312-B3/74. This reverted to proven Ferrari style with a tubular sub-structure, the driver's seat and fuel tanks were moved further forward to improve weight distri-

mula 1, and to sign up the Austrian Niki Lauda and the Swiss Clay Regazzoni as drivers.

For all their efforts, 1974 proved disappointing to Italy. Time after time the red cars proved fastest on the circuits, Lauda gaining pole starting position *nine* times and leading many races, but trouble struck too often and he only won two, the Spanish and Dutch GPs. Regazzoni added the German GP, and good places in other rounds made him second to McLaren driver Fittipaldi in the World Championship. But three wins were an improvement on none, and 1975 brought further improved Ferraris. The engine now gave 485 bhp, some 20 bhp more than the rival Cosworth-Ford though weighing only 5 lb more; weight distribution was again improved, a persistent understeer eradicated, the brakes enlarged, wheelbase and track modified, and the nose narrowed. Finally, with use of a de Dion-type rear axle

Ferrari used the flanks of their 312 monocoque to house ingenious cooling systems for oil and water. The oil radiators, vented at the top, were located forward in a low-pressure area, the water radiators are adjacent to the engine just ahead of the rear wheels, while between the two a NACA duct directs cool air to the exhaust system, shrouded under the engine

Power in situ: the engine's low position was very advantageous to the centre of gravity of the car. The neat cast-alloy cross member which also helps to support the engine subframe and five-speed gearbox can be seen, also the fibreglass air ducts to the inboard rear disc brakes

bution, while the suspension, handling and aerodynamics were all refined, and weight reduced. Power from the flat-12 went up to 480 bhp at 12 200 rpm, with a broader power band which notably improved acceleration from slow and middle-speed corners. Comm. Ferrari's final steps to raise his proud cars from the ruck were to withdraw from sports car racing in order to concentrate on For-

proposed, an excellent new transverse five-speed gearbox between the engine and final drive was fitted, the cars becoming the Tipo 312 T for *trasversale*.

Ferrari's private test circuit at Fiorano played a vital part in their development. Elaborate timing facilities, television cameras permitting the study of car behaviour under varied conditions, and a battery of computers

Swiss driver Clay Regazzoni en route to victory in the first US GP West, America's new Monaco-style street race at Long Beach, California, in March 1976. His 1975-type Ferrari 312T is wearing the high cold air box above the engine, this being the last race in which it was permitted

Opposite: *later in 1976 air for the engine was taken in through ducts in the double-skinned cockpit surround, shown clearly* (top) *in this photograph of Regazzoni's car at Monaco. This race was won in true champion's style by Lauda* (bottom)

made accurate testing and setting-up possible in advance of a race. The indefatigable Lauda put in prodigious hours of driving at Fiorano, the effort paying off handsomely. The Austrian repeated his 1974 feat of nine pole positions, but this time he won five of the races – the Monaco, Belgian, Swedish, French and US GPs, and scored in seven other GPs to become a deserving World Champion. Regazzoni contributed the Italian GP plus several places, and Ferrari won the Constructors' Championship hands down. Intruding further on Ford territory, Lauda also won the International Trophy at Silverstone and Regazzoni became the first Swiss to win a 'Swiss' GP – on French soil.

For 1976 the 312T-2 emerged, still smaller, lighter and cleaner, but minus the proposed de Dion axle. The power curve now showed a peak 500bhp at 12200rpm, but the engines were tuned to ensure maximum torque between 6700 and 13000rpm. Monocoque changes to meet new 1976 rules brought neat flush 'nostrils' set each side of the cockpit cowl to help the lusty flat-12s to breathe without the now-banned airboxes. While these cars were being completed, the older 312Ts achieved 100 per cent success in the first three 1976 races, Lauda taking the Brazil and South

African GPs and Regazzoni the new US GP West in California.

Lauda next placed second in the Spanish GP despite having injured ribs after a tractor accident in his own garden. He went on to win the Belgian and Monaco GPs, and next ran second to James Hunt's McLaren in the controversial British GP. Ferrari protested at a contravention of the rules, and Hunt's win was later disallowed, giving Lauda the victor's nine points. In the German GP at the Nürburgring Niki Lauda suffered serious burns when his 312T-2 slid off at a corner. Ferrari withdrew from the subsequent Austrian GP but allowed Regazzoni to contest the Dutch round, where he finished second. There followed a protest-ridden Italian GP at Monza, wherein the plucky Lauda returned to racing and finished fourth.

The final three World Championship rounds in Canada, the United States and Japan were disappointing for the dedicated Austrian, producing a third, an eighth and a retirement, making him a gallant loser by one point to McLaren driver James Hunt. But thanks to the combined efforts of Lauda and Regazzoni throughout the season, Ferrari retained the Constructors' Championship for 1976.

Specification

Engine
Twelve cylinders at 180 degrees; bore and stroke, 80 × 49·6mm; capacity, 2991·8cc; four overhead camshafts operating four valves per cylinder; Lucas fuel injection; Marelli-Dinoplex transistorised ignition; maximum power, 485bhp at 12200rpm, rising to approximately 500bhp in 1976.

Transmission
Ferrari five-speed transverse gearbox.

Chassis
Monocoque with tubular sub-structure; engine as stressed member. Front suspension by double wishbones and inboard coil spring/Koni damper units. Rear suspension by parallel lower links, single top links, twin radius arms and outboard coil spring/Koni damper units. Lockheed disc brakes, outboard front, inboard rear. Goodyear tyres.

Dimensions
Wheelbase, 8ft 3·1in; front track, 4ft 11·5in; rear track, 5ft 0·2in; Formula weight, 1287lb in 1975, 1270lb in 1976.

McLaren-Ford M23

'Perhaps the car is not the best. I can't say for sure, but the *team* is fantastic.'

Emerson Fittipaldi, 'Autocourse'

Three wins in 1973, its first season, augured well for the Coppuck-designed McLaren-Ford M23 sponsored by Yardley. The American Peter Revson, seen here in the International Trophy race at Silverstone, won the 1973 British GP on the same course and also the Canadian GP, while Denny Hulme took the Swedish GP

When Jack Brabham left Coopers of Surbiton in 1961 to become a driver/manufacturer, his place as number one in the racing team was taken by the young New Zealander Bruce McLaren. As a talented and highly methodical engineer, however, McLaren also felt the urge to make and race his own cars. He achieved his aim by 1965, and a year later had built his first Formula 1 car, the M2B. Ten years later the McLaren was a strongly established marque in the Grand Prix world, with over two dozen F1 victories and a double World Championship title to its credit. The saddest part of the McLaren story is that its brilliant founder was killed while testing at Goodwood in 1970, but the high example he set in practical design, untiring development and sound organisation has been faithfully carried on by his successors.

Appropriately, when the Colnbrook-based team scored its first F1 success in 1968, it was 'the Guvnor', Bruce himself, who won the Race of Champions at Brands Hatch with the first Cosworth-engined McLaren. This was the M7A, designed by Robin Herd and distinctive in the team's racing colour, bright orange. Fellow New Zealander Denny Hulme then won the BRDC Silverstone with Bruce second, after which three rousing Grand Prix wins in Belgium, Italy and Canada confirmed the young marque's 'arrival' in no mean manner. Preoccupation with those lucrative American events, the CanAm Cup series for Group 7 sports prototypes and the Indianapolis 500 Miles, restricted Grand Prix successes during the next four years, but they reaped rich recompense.

Following the Indianapolis trail set by Cooper, Lotus and Lola, McLaren Racing

The ubiquitous Cosworth-Ford DFV V8 engine, neatly installed in the M23 monocoque, seen in 1974 form when Marlboro and Texaco took over sponsorship of the team and McLaren driver Emerson Fittipaldi won his second World Championship title

Continuous development wrought subtle changes to the M23. In this 1975 view at Zolder, Belgium, the fuel-injection trumpets are turned inward; the effective but inelegant rear cross-member of angled section highlights the lack of a Maranello-style foundry

took a strong second place in the 1971 500, and then became the third British make to win outright when Mark Donohue led home in 1972 with a car entered by Roger Penske. Both McLarens were Offenhauser-powered M16s designed by Gordon Coppuck; they followed the Lotus 72 example in having slim chisel noses, side radiators and wedge shapes, and after their Indianapolis per-formances Coppuck employed the basic design features in a new Formula 1 car for 1973, the M23. This was a clean, incisive design to the customary Cosworth-plus-Hewland formula, with a neat monocoque sharing chassis stresses with the engine, a front-end combination of rising rate inboard suspension and Lockheed outboard disc brakes, and the reverse order, outboard suspension and inboard discs, at the rear.

When several Cosworth-powered teams were on an almost equal performance footing, McLaren's main assets were sound precision manufacture, meticulous chassis tuning, good team direction and driver talent. The Cosworth-Ford DFV engines were prepared by John Nicholson of Nicholson McLaren Ltd, a subsidiary enterprise based in nearby Hounslow, and the team was sponsored by the Yardley perfume house which had backed BRM until 1972. After a fifth place first time out in South Africa, the Yardley McLaren M23s scored three 1973 Championship race wins: the Swedish GP by Hulme, and the British and Canadian GPs by the American Peter Revson. For 1974 designer Coppuck wrought sundry suspension improvements, while the nose, airbox and rear wing were all modified. There were sponsorship changes too, the factory cars becoming 'Marlboro Team Texaco' entries, backed jointly by Philip Morris, makers of Marlboro cigarettes, and the Texaco fuel and oil concern. Thus the Yardley white, which had replaced the McLaren orange, was itself replaced by a red and white livery.

Drivers for 1974 were Denny Hulme and the brilliant Brazilian, Emerson Fittipaldi, who put in a cool and calculated season of points-earning to reap the highest rewards for driver and constructor. The year began well with Hulme's Argentine GP win, after which Fittipaldi weighed in with victory in the Championship GPs of Brazil, Belgium and Canada, plus another in a non-points GP at Brazilia. The intense competitiveness of the rival teams that season produced a cliffhanger Championship finale at Watkins Glen, USA, where a seemingly modest but sage fourth place clinched the two world titles for Fittipaldi the driver and McLaren the manufacturer. Adding Johnny Rutherford's great victory at Indianapolis with the works McLaren-Offenhauser M16C, and further USAC race wins at Ontario, Milwaukee and in the Pocono 500, and 1974 was indeed McLaren's golden year.

1975 was less pleasing. Hulme retired, the German Jochen Mass taking his place alongside Fittipaldi. The cars were plagued by handling problems which changed from understeer to oversteer before the right balance was achieved. But Fittipaldi won the Argentine and British GPs and garnered

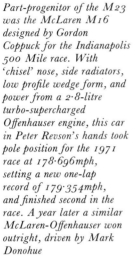

Part-progenitor of the M23 was the McLaren M16 designed by Gordon Coppuck for the Indianapolis 500 Mile race. With 'chisel' nose, side radiators, low profile wedge form, and power from a 2·8-litre turbo-supercharged Offenhauser engine, this car in Peter Revson's hands took pole position for the 1971 race at 178·696mph, setting a new one-lap record of 179·354mph, and finished second in the race. A year later a similar McLaren-Offenhauser won outright, driven by Mark Donohue

A Brazilian at home: 1974 World Champion Emerson Fittipaldi taking second place in the 1975 GP of Brazil at Interlagos with the Texaco/Marlboro-sponsored McLaren-Ford M23

A race the leader lost: James Hunt's M23 at the controversial 1976 British GP at Brands Hatch. Involved in a lap 1 shunt, the car was repaired in time for a re-start and led the race throughout, only to suffer subsequent disqualification. The twin air intakes conforming to 1976 rules and flexible plastic 'skirts' on the monocoque sides, aimed at improving aerodynamic efficiency, are fitted

sufficient points elsewhere to become runner-up to Ferrari driver Niki Lauda in the World Championship, while Mass emerged a surprised winner of the trouble-fraught Spanish GP, stopped after only 68 miles because of accidents.

When Emerson Fittipaldi left Marlboro Team Texaco to drive the Brazilian Copersucar in 1976, team chief Teddy Mayer signed up Englishman James Hunt, whose ability to 'tiger' in a Hesketh was happily transferred to a McLaren cockpit alongside Mass. Coppuck's faithful M23 served on, now with a Colnbrook-developed six-speed version of the Hewland gearbox, the car refined in aerodynamics and submitted to a weight-paring blitz. At least 30lb was saved in the suspension, body panels and by use of a compressed-air starter, operated by an air-line from the pits and thereby permitting a lighter battery.

The 1976 Championship season proved one of the most tense for many years. The mettlesome Hunt warmed up by collecting both the Race of Champions and the BRDC Silverstone, and then won Championship rounds in Spain, France, Britain, Germany and Holland. Unfortunately the racing was clouded by acrimony, controversy and an excess of protests; Hunt's British GP win was ruled out and at Monza his McLaren was relegated to the back row of the grid for allegedly practising with 101·6 octane fuel instead of the legal 101 octane. He did not finish, but more than made up for it by winning both the Canadian and United States Grands Prix. This made the final round at Fuji in Japan decisive, and Hunt's third place clinched the Championship title for him by one point over Ferrari driver Niki Lauda – a splendid combined achievement by the British driver and the McLaren stable with their basically four-year-old M23 Formula 1 design.

This overhead view of James Hunt in his McLaren, winning the 1976 Canadian GP at Mosport, shows the inboard front suspension with fabricated top rocker arms, disposition of the side radiators, and the incisive, purposeful shape of the M23

Specification
Engine
Cosworth-Ford DFV 90 degree V8; bore and stroke, 85·7 × 64·8mm; capacity, 2993cc; four overhead cam-shafts, two per bank, operating four valves per cylinder; Lucas fuel injection; Lucas Opus transistorised ignition; maximum power, 460bhp at 10250rpm, rising to 465bhp at 10500rpm in 1975.

Transmission
Hewland FG400 five-speed gearbox (six-speed in 1976); ZF differential.

Chassis
Monocoque with stress-bearing engine. Side radiators. Front suspension by double wishbones and inboard coil spring/damper units. Rear suspension by lower wishbones, single top links, twin radius rods and outboard coil spring/damper units. Lockheed disc brakes, outboard front, inboard rear. Goodyear tyres.

Dimensions
Wheelbase, 8ft 8·2in, 8ft 11in in 1975-76; front track, 5ft 4·2in; rear track, 5ft 6in; Formula weight, 1270lb.